LITERATURE ANTHOLOGIES

**A Collection of Prose and Poetry
on the Theme of**

RELATIONSHIPS

Edited by
Michael Spring
Editor, Literary Cavalcade

SCHOLASTIC INC.

CURRICULUM CONSULTANTS

Ms. Jo-Ann Lynn Mullen
Associate Professor of Education
Assistant Director, Division of
Education Studies
University of Northern Colorado
Greeley, Colorado

Ms. Gaylene Pepe
Department Head, English
Colonia Senior High School
Colonia, New Jersey

STAFF

Editorial Director:	Eleanor Angeles
Project Editor:	Michael Spring
Art Director:	Joe Borzetta
Assistant Editor:	Bette Birnbaum
Contributing Consultant:	Adrienne Betz
Editorial Assistant:	Karen Salazar

COVER ART: "Le Bouquet" by Pablo Picasso, 1958. Editions Combat pour la Paix.

ISBN 0-590-34582-6

ACKNOWLEDGMENTS

Grateful acknowledgment is made to the following authors and publishers for the use of copyrighted materials. Every effort has been made to obtain permission to use previously published material. Any errors or omissions are unintentional.

Atheneum Publishers, Inc. for "Herbert Hahn" from AND MORE BY ANDY ROONEY by Andy Rooney. Copyright © 1982 Essay Productions.
The Baltimore Sun for "Calvin: A Boy of Unusual Vision" by Alice Steinbach. Copyright © 1984 by *The Baltimore Sun*.
Delacorte Press for DEAR BILL, REMEMBER ME? AND OTHER STORIES by Norma Fox Mazer. Copyright © 1976 by Norma Fox Mazer.
Delacorte Press/Seymour Lawrence for "The Kid Nobody Could Handle," excerpted from the book WELCOME TO THE MONKEY HOUSE by Kurt Vonnegut, Jr. Copyright © 1955 by Kurt Vonnegut, Jr. Originally published in SATURDAY EVENING POST.
Paul Engle for "Together." Copyright © 1985 by Paul Engle.
Mari Evans for "If There Be Sorrow" from I AM A BLACK WOMAN by Mari Evans, copyright © 1970 by Mari Evans.
Edward Field for "The Telephone" by Edward Field.
Elaine Greenspan for "Fat Chance" by Elaine Greenspan.
Harcourt Brace Jovanovich, Inc. for "In Search of Our Mothers' Gardens" from IN SEARCH OF OUR MOTHERS' GARDENS by Alice Walker. Copyright © 1974 by Alice Walker. "Road to the Isles" reprinted from CRESS DELAHANTY by Jessamyn West. Copyright 1948, 1976 by Jessamyn West.
David Huddle for "Icicle." First appeared in *Mid-American Review*, Vol. I, No. I. Copyright © 1984 by David Huddle.
Dykeman Kleihauer and **Lenninger Literary Agency** for "The Cub" by Dykeman Kleihauer, copyright © 1953 by Crowell-Collier Company.
Houghton Mifflin Company for "A Sprig of Rosemary" from THE COMPLETE POETICAL WORKS OF AMY LOWELL. Copyright © 1955 by Houghton Mifflin Company. Copyright © 1983 renewed by Houghton Mifflin Company, Brinton P. Roberts, Esquire, and G. d'Andelot Belin, Esquire.
McGraw-Hill Book Company for "You Don't Love Me," excerpted from IF LIFE IS A BOWL OF CHERRIES, WHAT AM I DOING IN THE PITS? Copyright © 1971, 1972, 1973, 1974, 1975, 1976, 1977, 1978 by Erma Bombeck. All rights reserved.
William Morrow & Company for "You Came, Too" from BLACK FEELING, BLACK TALK, BLACK JUDGMENT by Nikki Giovanni. Copyright © 1968, 1970 by Nikki Giovanni.
Harold Ober Associates Incorporated for "Thank You, M'am" by Langston Hughes. Copyright 1958 by Langston Hughes.
Random House, Inc. for "The House Dog's Grave," reprinted from SELECTED POEMS by Robinson Jeffers. Copyright 1941 by Robinson Jeffers.
Real People Press for "Notes to Myself: Relationships" from NOTES TO MYSELF by Hugh Prather. © 1970 Real People Press.
Norman Rosten for "Jumpy" from UNDER THE BOARDWALK by Norman Rosten, published by Prentice-Hall, Inc. Copyright © 1968 by Norman Rosten.
St. Luke's Press for "Motheroot" by Marilou Awiakta. Reprinted from ABIDING APPALACHIA.
St. Martin's Press, Incorporated and **The Reader's Digest Association, Inc.** for "A Kitten for Mrs. Ainsworth," reprinted from the book, THE BEST OF JAMES HERRIOT, copyright © 1982 by The Reader's Digest Association, Inc; copyright © 1976, 1977 by James Herriot.
Scholastic Inc. for "Life Without Father" by Kristin Lems. "Growing Older" by Julie Lochnicht. "The Tree" by Linda Marasco. "Making Potica" by Tina Pomeroy. "Aunt Sarah Died One Summer Night" by Lisa Hirschboeck.
Charles Scribner's Sons for "A Mother in Mannville" from WHEN THE WHIPPOORWILL by Marjorie Kinnan Rawlings. Copyright © 1940 by Marjorie Kinnan Rawlings; copyright renewed © 1968 Norton Baskin.
Simon & Schuster, Inc. for "The Big Deal" from TELEVISION PLAYS by Paddy Chayefsky. Copyright © 1955 by Paddy Chayefsky, renewed © 1983 by Susan Chayefsky.
Jesse Stuart Foundation, H. Edward Richardson, Editor-in-Chief, University of Louisville, Louisville, Kentucky 40292 for an excerpt from "God's Oddling" from A JESSE STUART READER, copyright © 1963.
Jim Tolley for "The Daymarker." Copyright © 1985 by James Tolley.
University of Georgia Press for "Poem of the Mother" from THE SCIENCE OF GOODBYES by Myra Sklarew, published in 1982 and reprinted in 1983.
University of Pittsburgh Press for "Oranges" from BLACK HAIR by Gary Soto. Copyright © 1985 by Gary Soto.
Viking Penguin Inc. for "Breakfast" from THE LONG VALLEY by John Steinbeck. Copyright © 1938, renewed © 1966 by John Steinbeck.
Margaret Walker for "Lineage" from the book FOR MY PEOPLE, published by Yale University Press, 1942. Copyright by Margaret Walker Alexander.

ILLUSTRATION AND PHOTOGRAPHY CREDITS

Ken Hamilton 6, 10. Time Inc. 12. Mel Williges 14, 19, 22, 27, 30, 80, 112, 119, 120, 174. Arthur Tress 16. David Lorczak/Scholastic Photography Awards 34. The Baltimore Sun/Harp 36, 39, 42. Wayne Miller/Magnum 46. Eric Velasquez 50, 55. Phil Huling 58. Eve Arnold/Magnum 62. Jane Zwinger 64, 68, 73. Steve Moore 82, 124, 126, 150, 180. James Wojcik/Scholastic Photography Awards 86. Vincent Nasta 88, 92, 96, 101, 104. UPI 98. Steve Madson 132, 134, 139. Paul Caponigro 156. Greg Spalenka 158, 163, 166. Wide World Photos 178. Jack Delano 186. Bob Adelman/Magnum 190.

CONTENTS

POETRY

DRAMA

"I learned to love many of the things he loved."

Jesse Stuart

THE EARTH POET

● Jesse Stuart spent most of his life in Kentucky hill country, writing about the land and the people that he knew and loved. In this essay, he makes us see the unexpected genius of a poor farmer — his own father. As you read, think about what Jesse Stuart has learned from his father, and what his father has shared with him. Without this special relationship, Jesse might never have become a successful writer.

NOTHING EVER ESCAPED MY FATHER, FOR HE was an earth poet who loved the land and everything on it. He liked to watch things grow. From the time I was big enough for him to lead me by the hand, I went with him over the farm. If I couldn't walk all the way in those early days, he'd carry me on his back. I learned to love many of the things he loved.

Sometime in the dim past of my boyhood, my father unloaded me from his back under some white-oak trees just beginning to leaf. "Look at this hill, son," he said, gesturing broadly with a sweep of his hand. "Look up that steep hill toward the sky. See how pretty that new-ground corn is."

This was the first field I can remember my father's taking me to see. The rows of corn curved like dark green rainbows around a high slope with a valley and its little tributaries running down through the center. The corn blades rustled in the wind, and my father said he could understand what the corn blades were saying. He told me they whispered to each other, and this was hard for me to believe. I reasoned that before anything could speak or make a sound it had to have a mouth. When my father said the corn could talk, I got down on my knees and looked a stalk over.

"This corn hasn't got a mouth," I told my father. "How can anything talk when it doesn't have a mouth?"

He laughed like the wind in the corn and hugged me to his knees, and we went on.

The one thing my father brought me to see that delighted him most was the pumpkins. I'd never seen so many pumpkins with long necks and small bodies. Pumpkins as big around as the bottom of a flour barrel were sitting in the furrows[1] beneath the tall corn, immovable as rocks. There were pumpkins, and more pumpkins, of all colors — yellow and white, green and brown.

"Look at this, won't you," my father said. "Look what corn, what beans, what pumpkins. Corn ears so big they lean the corn-stalks. Beans as thick as honey-locust beans on the honey-locust tree. And pumpkins thicker than the stumps in this new ground. I could walk all over this field on pumpkins and never step on the ground."

He looked upon the beauty of this cove he had cleared and his three crops growing here. He rarely figured a field in dollars and cents. Although he never wasted a dollar, money didn't mean everything to him. He liked to see the beauty of growing things on the land. He carried this beauty in his mind.

Once, when we were walking between cornfields on a rainy Sunday afternoon, he pointed to a redbird on its nest in a locust tree, a redbird with shiny red feathers against the dark background of a nest. It was just another bird's nest to me until he whispered, "Ever see anything as pretty as what the raindrops do to that redbird sitting on her dark nest?" From this day on, I have liked to see birds, especially redbirds, sitting on their nests in the rain. But my father was the one to make me see the beauty.

"A blacksnake is a pretty thing," he once said to me, "so shiny and black in the spring sun after he sheds his winter skin."

He was the first man I ever heard say a snake was pretty. I never forgot his saying it. I can even remember the sumac thicket where he saw the blacksnake.

He saw more beauty in trees than any man I have ever known. He would walk through a strange forest laying his hand upon the trees, saying this oak or that pine, that beech or poplar, was a beautiful tree. Then he would single out other trees and say they should be cut. He would always give his reasons for cutting a tree: too many trees on a root stool, too thick, one damaged by fire at the butt, one leaning against another, too many on the ground, or the soil not deep enough above a ledge of rocks to support them.

Then there were the hundreds of times my father took me to the hills to see wild flowers. I thought it was silly at first. He would sit on a dead log, maybe one covered with wild moss, somewhere under the tall beech trees, listening to the wind in the canopy of leaves above, looking at a clump of violets of percoon growing beside a rotted log. He could sit there enjoying himself indefinitely. Only when the sun went down would we get up and start for home. Father wouldn't break the Sabbath by working, except in an emergency. He would follow a cow that was overdue to calve. He would watch over ewes in the same manner. He followed them to the high cliffs and helped them deliver their lambs, saving their lives. He would do such things on Sundays, and he would fight forest fires. But he always said he could make a living working six days in the week. Yet he was restless on Sundays. He had to walk around and look over his fields and enjoy them.

My father didn't have to travel over the country searching for something beautiful to see. He didn't have to go away to find beauty, for he found it everywhere around him. He had eyes to find it. He had a mind to know it. He had a heart to appreciate it. He was an uneducated poet of this earth. And if anybody had told him that he was, he wouldn't have understood. He would have turned and walked away without saying anything.

In the winter, when snow was over the ground, and the stars glistened, he'd go to the barn to feed the livestock at four in the morning. I have seen him put corn in the feedboxes for the horses and mules, then go out and stand and look at the morning moon. He once told me he always kept a horse with a flaxen[2] mane and tail because he liked to see one run in the moonlight with his mane arched high and his tail floating on the wind.

When spring returned, he was always taking me someplace to show me a new tree he had found, or a pretty red mushroom growing on a rotting stump in some deep hollow. He found so many strange and beautiful things that I tried to rival him by making

"No one who really knew him ever felt sorry for my father."

discoveries, too. I looked into the out-of-the-way and unexpected places to find the beautiful and the unusual.

I didn't get the idea of dead leaves being golden ships on the sea from a storybook. And neither did my father, for he had never read a book in his life. He'd never had a book read to him either. It was in October, and we were sitting on the bank of W-Branch. We were watching the blue autumn water slide swiftly over the slate rocks. My father picked up leaves that were shaped like little ships and dropped them into the water.

"These are ships on swift water," he told me, "going to far-off lands where strangers will see them." He had a special love for autumn leaves, and he'd pick them up when we were out walking and ask me to identify them. He'd talk about how pretty each leaf was and how a leaf was prettier after it was dead than when it was alive and growing.

Many people thought my father was just a one-horse farmer who never got much out of life. They saw only a little man, dressed in clean, patched overalls, with callused and brier-scratched hands. They often saw the beard along his face. And they saw him go off and just stand in a field and look at something. They thought he was moody. Well, he was that all right, but when he was standing there and people thought he was looking into space, he was looking at a flower or a mushroom or a new bug he'd discovered for the first time. And when he looked up into a tree, he wasn't searching for a hornet's nest to burn or a bird's nest to rob. He wasn't trying to find a bee tree. He was just looking closely at the beauty in a tree. And among the millions, he always found one different enough to excite him.

No one who really knew him ever felt sorry for my father. Any feeling of pity turned to envy. For my father had a world of his own, larger and richer than the vast earth that world travelers know. He found more beauty in his acres and square miles than poets who have written a half-dozen books. Only my father couldn't write down the words to express his thoughts. He had no common symbols by which to share his wealth. He was a poet who lived his life upon this earth and never left a line of poetry — except to those of us who lived with him.

[1] **furrows:** trenches in the earth made by a plow
[2] **flaxen:** soft; pale; the color of straw

A CLOSER LOOK

1. What is an earth poet? How does a person become an earth poet?

2. In what ways was Jesse's father a well-educated person? In what ways was he not a well-educated person?

3. In what ways do this father and son seem close? In what ways are they not close? How do you think Jesse's father would have felt if he had been able to read this essay?

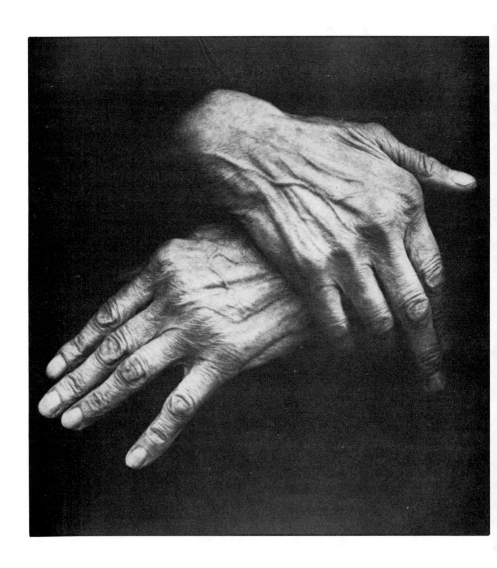

● Good friends become a part of one another. Even when they are separated, such friends remain with each other in memory. What do you remember about your distant friends? Probably the exact same things that you love most about them.

Amy Lowell

A SPRIG OF ROSEMARY

I cannot see your face.
When I think of you,
It is your hands which I see.
Your hands
Sewing,
Holding a book,
Resting for a moment on the sill of a window.
My eyes keep always the sight of your hands,
But my heart holds the sound of your voice
And the soft brightness which is your soul.

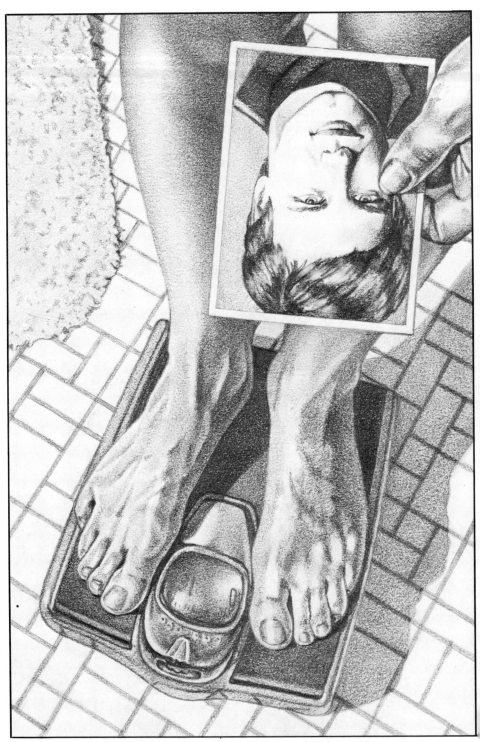

"My mother calls me pleasantly plump."

Elaine Greenspan

FAT CHANCE

• Before you can form strong relationships with other people, it's important to know who you are yourself. And if you want others to like you, it helps if you like yourself, too. This story is about a teenage girl who has more going for her than she realizes.

WHEN I BITE INTO A HOT DOG (124 CALORIES) and a bun (119 calories), guilt dilutes the pleasure of the juicy meat breaking on my tongue. That's because I am . . . uh . . . overweight. Like . . . fat.

Not just five or ten pounds, what other girls constantly fuss about, but genuinely overweight.

My mother calls me pleasantly plump. It is not pleasant, and it is not plump. It is fat. I am also only five feet three, so I look like a tea kettle. I won't say how much I weigh. No one knows. But my weight is the first thing you notice about me if we should meet. I see how people look me over and then try to concentrate on my face.

So how come, on this lovely April Thursday, I am sitting — roly-poly Becky Bowen — in the Taft High School cafeteria with Tanner Simmons, Student Council president, six feet of blond, blue-eyed brawn?

"It's insanity that the delegates want to buy a bronze tiger for the media center, Becky. The school already has one in the gym and one on the patio. Come on, Madam Secretary, what should we do?"

15

"Prepare a position paper. Point out that people are scared to come up at night for games and dances because it's so dark. The two thousand dollars we raised should be spent on parking-lot lights. Explain that the administration has no money to do it."

Tanner listens, his blue eyes concentrating. This has the effect of melting my bones, the only thin part of me. When he leans back to catch the crushed ice in his Pepsi, I study his throat.

"But the kids are bored with the idea of lights," Tanner warns. "They want to leave something glamorous." A strategy session with Tanner stimulates my feelings for him, but it's the pits for my ego. Tanner likes and, politically, needs me, but he has a girlfriend: Jill Walker. Five feet seven. A size six.

"If we get a coalition, you could swing the votes," I tell him. "I've done a head count. Most of the seniors will come over. So will the juniors, once they hear the arguments properly presented. It's just the ninth and tenth graders who go gaga over a tiger. But if you call for a straw vote and they see which way the wind is blowing, we can blitz them."

"OK. Draw up a list of reasons in favor of the lights. Simplified, so some of those cretins can understand. You're good at doing that." He smiles, buttering me up. Tanner can't write worth a darn, yet put him in front of the student body and he could talk them into two-hour study halls.

"I'll write it this weekend."

"What would I do without you, Becky?" He flips his empty cup into a wastebasket and then looks across the cafeteria to Jill and her friends. Thin friends. All in Calvin Klein straight denim skirts and skintight T-shirts.

"Is that it?" Tanner asks, his eyes on Jill.

I slam my notebook shut. "Yes," I snap.

"Be sure and get that list of reasons to me Monday. Boy, will I have a hot speech ready next Friday."

And he is gone, over to Jill.

As I walk out of the cafeteria, I feel people are watching my fat jiggle. Actually, I don't jiggle at all, but I'm afraid I might start. My mother tells me I have large bones. My father says I have such a pretty face. Other people say I'm built solid. Or that I'll outgrow it. That's how you know you're fat, when people say those things.

I read diets all the time. I have put myself on 1,000 calories a day, following menus I find in women's magazines. But who can live on skim milk, bouillon, cottage cheese, and fish? It's not real food. Real food is french fries, homemade bread and sweet butter, and Haagen-Dazs coffee ice cream. That's what the rest of the world lives on.

Sometimes I'll lose three pounds after a heroic two-week struggle with yogurt and tuna. I shift around on the scale, or stand on one foot, hoping to force the number down. Soon, I go off the diet and gain back the three pounds.

Today, walking home after school, I think about the way Tanner looked at Jill and I feel sorry for myself.

I head straight for the pantry, even though I tell my mother not to buy sweets. My father says why should he suffer on my account, so my mother compromises and keeps one jar of strawberry jam hidden behind the cereal boxes.

I spread the glistening painkiller on two slices of bread and wolf it down with milk.

At first I feel soothed. Why shouldn't I too have my pleasures, just like everyone else? This feeling lasts about the three minutes it takes to swallow everything.

Then I loathe myself. *How could I have been so weak? The jam didn't even taste that good. Why must I eat when I'm depressed? Don't I know that I only get more depressed?*

I go into my parents' bedroom. On the wall in living color hangs the Student Council picture of me, Tanner, and the two other officers taken for the yearbook. We are standing outside in front of the Taft tiger. The treasurer and vice-president, two thin girls, are flanking Tanner. I stand in front of them, so the full force of my body is there for the world to see. I am wearing a blue sweater and skirt, and I look like a mountain. The two girls could both fit in my skirt. Tanner's lean body is completely covered by my girth.

Twenty years from now when I open my yearbook this is the memory I'll have of myself.

I take down the picture and hide it in my bedroom closet. Then I rush into the kitchen, grab the strawberry jam, and throw it into the outside garbage can.

Monday night Tanner telephones. "Where were you first period?

17

Did you write the speech?''

I had been late to school and did not stop by his locker.

"Yes, it's finished. I pointed out that a school is built on more than athletic symbols like the tiger. For example, people should feel safe when they drive up to school for night activities. Otherwise they won't come. Lights will draw crowds for all kinds of events. I said that the parking-lot lights will shine like a timeless beacon of school spirit.''

"Wow! Great stuff, Becky. You bring a tear to my eye. Is it all written out so I can just deliver it?''

"Yes.''

"You should run for next year's president. Jill agrees that you're a natural politician.''

I did not want to hear what Jill thought about my political talents. "It should take about ten minutes to deliver. That's the Council's attention span.''

"Super. Wait until I tell Jill that line about a timeless beacon of school spirit. The troops will love it!'' He hangs up before I say good-bye. Tanner's vanity is supreme. He probably already believes he thought up the speech himself. Yet he has been a competent president. I should know. I have been active in student government since the sixth grade. I don't feel self-conscious about my weight when I'm arguing for student rights or planning fund-raising projects.

I go into the hall where there is a full-length mirror, and study myself ruthlessly. The face is not bad. Brown, thick hair. Nice blue eyes. Terrific nose. Excellent skin. No zits.

But the body!

While I don't have the kind of fat that hangs over jeans, still I am broad in the hips and shoulders. In the summer I never wear shorts. My thighs are too heavy. Compared to the popular girls at Taft like Jill, I look gross.

It's one of those nights when I decide yet again to take steps. I clip a discount coupon I saw in the evening paper advertising a new health club, borrow my mom's car, and check it out. I have been to various weight clubs and exercise classes, but I can never hang in long enough to lose real weight.

I find the Atlas Health Club tucked into a seedy shopping center

"I suppose you wanna look skinny?"

off Menaul Boulevard. Lots of young mother types are working out on the machines, their toddlers playing nearby. It's nothing like the intimidating big health clubs where I feel conspicuous even walking in.

I hand over my coupon and write out a check for two months' membership. The woman who owns the place, Mrs. Ferguson, is about forty years old and kind of lumpy-looking in her tights. This makes me feel better. In Nautilus or Tom Young's, everybody is so thin you wonder how it's possible to look like that and still be alive.

Mrs. Ferguson writes out my membership card. Then she points to the machines where women are working on various parts of their bodies.

"Hey, Gino, here's another new customer." She pats my shoulder. "Go ahead, sweetheart. Gino will turn you into Brooke Shields."

The person who heads my way is not walking the way walking is generally managed. He seems to be slithering. He has an extraordinary body. I can't take my eyes off his body. It is an astonishing creation.

He studies my card.

"Beck Bowen, huh?" He reaches out to shake my hand. "I'm Gino Puglisi." I put out my hand and stare as it is swallowed up in a large paw.

"You think I look weird?" he asks.

"No . . . o . . . I just never saw anyone so . . ."

"Perfect? Sublime? MONSTROUS?" He breaks into a loud laugh.

Gino Puglisi is about my height, maybe an inch taller, say five feet four. Dressed in black shorts and black tank top, his body is hugely overdeveloped. The shoulders and arms are gigantic, rippling muscles. He has a thick neck. Although his waist and hips are small, the thighs and calves bulge with muscle.

"You ain't never seen a bodybuilder before?" he asks.

"Only in magazines."

"I been weightlifting since high school. Look, I'm short. I couldn't try out for basketball, right?" He bursts into another hoarse laugh, showing even white teeth against olive skin. His black curly hair is cut very short. This makes the head look almost dainty above the body bursting below like a ripe flower.

He strikes a pose, his arms raised above his head, the fists clenched so that the muscles spring out, while the legs are bent and turn sideways.

"Last year I won first prize for biceps definition," he says.

"That's nice."

"You could look like this . . . Betty, baby."

"Becky. Becky Bowen. I'm not a baby and I have no desire to look like that."

He drops his pose and stands normally. "Sorry. I was just joking, Becky." He studies me. "I'll bet you worry about being a fatty."

"I didn't come in here to be insulted. You don't look exactly normal yourself."

"No harm meant. It ain't no disgrace to have flesh on your bones. You in high school? I remember what a shnook I felt. I was heavy, plus being short."

"I'm very active in school," I tell him. I don't care for the too-friendly way he talks to me.

"That's good. Say, you could have a great body." He squeezes my arm. "You ain't soft."

I pull my arm back from his grasp.

"You just gotta work out, switch to the right kinds of food. I gotta protein drink you'll love. And a rye germ oil that keeps you from cravin' sugar. And raw almonds. For energy."

"It sounds disgusting," I tell him.

He ignores my comments and takes me over to the exercise machines, where he shows me how they work on different parts of the body. Three nights a week he helps Mrs. Ferguson, he says, and during the day he is majoring in architecture at the university. That surprises me.

He helps me with the machines, adjusting bars, showing me how to lie flat for the leg lifts, reminding me to breathe. An hour passes quickly.

"You feel better?" he asks when I am finished.

"Yes. But I'll never be able to lose all the weight I want to lose."

"I suppose you wanna look skinny?"

"Sure."

"That's a fantasy. You ain't never gonna look like one of them models."

I resent his analysis of what I fantasize about — although it happens to be true.

He strikes another pose. "You should be proud of the body you got. Or the one you're gonna get." This time he crosses his wrists in front of his torso and leans forward. As if called, the muscles leap out from all over his body. Actually, I think this looks disgusting, but I say nothing.

I start going to Atlas three nights a week. Gino gets me using weights after a session on the machines. I start with barbells, lying flat and lifting them with my arms.

"Ten more reps. Breathe! Breathe!" Gino yells. He takes a special interest in my case. Of course, I have a well-developed conversational facility with guys. You can't flirt, you find another way to communicate.

Gino advises me not to waste my hunger on empty calories. He gives me bottles of his homemade protein drink. It tastes pretty good. I can't stand to use the rye germ oil he gives me, however. It smells faintly sour. I also begin cutting up tofu for salads.

In two weeks I lose several pounds, but I don't discuss this with anyone. I also feel better and have more energy.

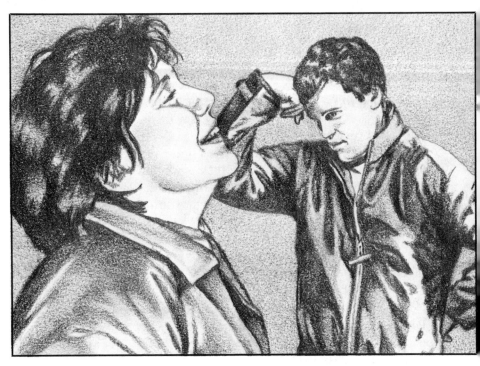

"Last year I won first prize for biceps definition."

At school Tanner delivers the speech I wrote. He has studied it for several days and barely glances down at the paper when he speaks. When the vote is taken, we win. The Student Council votes to buy lights for the parking lot. The *Taft Tattler* writes a nasty editorial, mocking us for presenting the school with such a boring gift. But we don't care. We know we're right.

In late April we watch the tall lights being trucked into the parking lot. Tanner hugs and kisses me. My heart quivers. Jill is there too, smiling.

"Becky, you're a pro. Tanner could never have swung the Council without the speech you wrote."

I disentangle myself from Tanner and thank her. What can I tell you? Jill Walker is a nice person. Even if she is thin, has a dozen Ralph Lauren shirts, and drives her own Jeep.

Jill, Tanner, and I celebrate with an after-school libation[1] in the snack bar. They drink root-beer floats. I have a carton of skim milk.

"Are you on a diet?" Jill asks.

"I've lost a few pounds."

"There's something different about you," Tanner muses.

I remain silent. Pretty soon they walk off together, their arms wrapped around each other's waists. Watching them, I eat a few of the raw almonds I now keep in my backpack. To console myself.

"Lift! Come on! Lift! You can do it!"

"I'm trying," I gasp. I am attempting to lift a large steel barbell Gino has brought into the center. No matter how hard I tug, the weight doesn't budge.

Gino walks over and lifts the hundred-pound barbell as if it were light plastic.

"Try again," he orders.

I bend to the weight, gripping the bar, straining, blocking out all thoughts of the world, and lift. The bar comes up inch by inch. I get it to my waist and then I drop it on the wooden floor.

"Not bad," Gino concedes.

Pumping iron is what Gino informs me I'm doing. I have lost six pounds since I started at Atlas a month ago, but mainly I'm getting stronger.

"I don't want a neck like yours," I tell Gino. "And I want my arms and thighs to look normal, not like a workhorse." Which is what you look like, I almost add.

Gino laughs. He always laughs when I needle him about his body. That irritates me. He's so smug, I can't get at him.

"I ain't letting you develop a neck like mine. And your legs'll look like legs is supposed to look. Strong. For doing their job. Form follows function. That's what I believe."

"I know that saying. It comes from architecture."

"You surprised I know that? You think I don't know nothin'? That I'm an illiterate jock that's just into bodybuilding?"

"Don't be so defensive. I never said that." Actually, it's just what I think about Gino. He is kind of a working-class person. The way he looks. The way he talks.

We're the last ones to leave the health center. Gino stalks off to his car angrily, walking close to the ground like some powerful animal.

"You won," Tanner announces. The June election for next year's officers is over, and I have been elected Student Council president. Tanner and Jill are graduating seniors. I'm a junior. I gave a good campaign speech. I said it was no use complaining about student apathy, that instead the Student Council should press for change on specific issues. First, we should ask that assemblies be scheduled during the day instead of after school when no one comes. The way to develop school spirit is through well-attended assemblies. Next, I proposed regular meetings between the administration and a Student Council committee to redress[2] grievances. Finally, my hottest proposal was to turn the old library into a student center where kids could meet during their free time.

My opponent, Gordon Cowan, talked a lot of rah-rah nonsense about getting the football team a new mascot and how great Taft was. He never suggested anything specific. Kids aren't as apathetic as people think. Give them meaty issues and they opt for change.

My body is changing. Looking in the hall mirror, I see my stomach is flatter, my arms and legs are contoured. I'd like to be four inches taller and twenty pounds lighter, but that is wishful thinking. As Gino says, "You gotta go with the flow." Meaning, that I am who I am and that even if I dropped the weight I would eventually gain most of it back, unless I starved myself for life. Still, I have lost eight pounds and Gino thinks I could lose six or seven more to achieve a realistic base. I will still be a stocky person. But somehow "stocky" sounds more palatable[3] than "fat."

Several days after the election, while we are both on our Exercycles, I confide to Gino my feelings for Tanner.

"You gotta chance?"

"Never. That girlfriend of his is gorgeous, thin, and besides, she's very nice."

After ten miles we get down. Gino pours me a glass of high-protein drink from his thermos. It tastes of crushed pecans, wheat germ, and coconut.

"He said I looked different, though."

"Whadda I tell you?"

"There's no way I'll ever have someone like Tanner fall for me," I sigh. "I'll never be glamorous and thin."

I am covered with sweat from my workout, but Gino's skin is smooth and dry. He does his serious workouts at the university gym.

"The trouble with you, Becky, is you got no confidence in yourself. This guy sounds like a nerd. Once you told me how you wrote his speeches for him."

"He's not a nerd. Don't talk like that."

"He ain't no brain, that's for sure."

"Speaking of brains, did anyone ever tell you what a double negative is? Do you speak that way at the university?"

"Sure. I ain't out to impress nobody."

"I'll second that."

Gino stands up, grasps his hands in front of his chest, and bends one leg, a fierce look on his face. All the biceps, triceps, and veins bulge into sharp definition.

I have seen him do this and many other exhibition poses lots of times by now. I am bored.

"If only Tanner would realize how my political temperament suits his," I murmur, thinking out loud.

Gino drops his pose and glares at me. He puts on his sweats and starts for the door. Mrs. Ferguson looks up from the front desk. "Hey, Gino, isn't it a bit early for you to leave?" He does not look back. He slams the glass door behind him. I shower, change into jeans, and drive home, thinking that maybe Tanner will notice me when I lose five more pounds.

The next time I come to exercise, Gino is not around. Maybe he's doing a paper for class. He's never sick. I ask Mrs. Ferguson.

"Gino quit. You saw him flounce out the other night? Well, he calls me the next day to say he's too busy with school to work here any more. I don't know what got into that boy."

Without Gino to prod and encourage me on the machines and weights, how will I keep up my program? He was always there to give me a protein drink, to remind me to take vitamins and health food. I want to phone him, but who am I to intrude on his private life? Gino lives in another world. I am just a high school kid he helped for a while.

During the next week I lose my ambition for working out. I move through the exercise machines mechanically, not really pushing. I skip the Exercycle. Gino's weights are gone. Sometime when I wasn't there, he came and took them back, so there is no more pumping iron either.

I can feel my body softening along with my will.

"You shouldn't be eating that greasy hamburger," Tanner says Monday at lunch when we are working on the Student Council agenda.

"Why is it any of your business?"

"For a while there you were losing weight."

"Not really," I lie. "For your information I am a gross, fat female. I always have been and I always will be." I finish my hamburger (312 calories) and an orange soda (240 empty calories).

"Stop biting my head. I don't care if you're 200 pounds. You'd still be my friend. I couldn't have made it through the year without you, Becky. That's why I'm concerned. I care for you a lot."

"Humph. How about Jill?"

"Jill has nothing to do with this. I said you were my friend. Doesn't that count for anything?"

He takes my right hand and grasps it in both of his. He is looking directly at me. It is very funny that I feel no shiver at the body contact.

"Thanks, Tanner. You're an OK person."

"Don't let me interrupt anything," Jill says, coming up to us.

I stand up. "Hold onto Tanner, Jill. He's not a bad guy."

I walk away fast. I have a little cry. I blow my nose and leave campus, cutting Spanish. At home I borrow my mom's car and drive down to the university. Parking the car, I head for the architecture building. Gino once told me he has a study carrel on the third floor. I run up the steps to the library and cross a large, beautiful room. June sunlight streams in from clerestory[4] windows high above the books. At an oak carrel behind the stacks I recognize Gino's powerful back and the head with its dark, cropped curls. He is writing.

He looks up as I approach.

"You."

"Yes." He looks different. Older. He is wearing a yellow polo shirt and jeans.

"So? You been working out regular? Your arms look soft."

"You took the weights."

"That's right. I did."

"I've been eating junk food."

"Your friend Tanner notice you yet?"

"Not in that way."

Gino taps a pencil on the desk. He has another pencil behind his ears. I had never noticed how flat his ears lay against his head.

"I take down the picture and hide it in my bedroom closet."

"I miss you. I wish you'd come back and help me train."

He scratches his powerful neck and doesn't speak.

"When I do leg lifts I forget to breathe. I go tight and almost pass out."

"Let me get my stuff." Gino gathers up his papers and puts everything into a canvas gym bag. We walk across the library and down the stairs. Outside on the grass, Gino puts an arm around my shoulders.

"You ain't never gonna be thin, Becky. Real thin."

"I know."

"You ever gonna get over this guy Tanner?"

"I AM over him. That's what I want to talk to you about. And other things."

Gino studies me. Then he takes hold of my upper arm.

"Look at that. Blubber. That's what it's gonna be if you don't keep after it."

"I know."

"It ain't good to let yourself go. You eating your tofu?"

"I ain't."

He looks sharply at me. "You think that's funny, huh? A Student

27

Council president gotta talk good.''

I laugh. Gino does not even smile. He bites his lower lip. We are standing next to a small reflecting pool. Gino places one leg up on the pool edge and rests his elbow on the knee, his chin cupped in his hand. He looks like a Rodin[5] statue.

I put my leg up next to him and imitate his pose. We gaze at one another without speaking. He has dark brown eyes and heavy black lashes.

We remain like that, my calf muscles flexed to keep from moving, until two people step out of the architecture building, stop, and look in surprise at us.

[1] **libation:** drink
[2] **redress:** correct; remedy
[3] **palatable:** agreeable
[4] **clerestory:** an outside wall with windows that rises above a roof
[5] **Rodin, Auguste** (1840-1917): French sculptor, whose work includes "The Thinker"

A CLOSER LOOK

1. What causes Becky's life to change? What changes occur in her physically? What changes occur mentally?

2. Why do you think Becky is attracted to Tanner at the beginning of the story? Why is she attracted to Gino at the end?

3. If Becky were your friend, what advice would you give her about health, school, and her relationships with boys?

● Do relationships survive only away from crowds? We surround ourselves with people, but only when we find someone who loves and understands us are we not alone.

Nikki Giovanni

YOU CAME, TOO

I came to the crowd seeking friends
I came to the crowd seeking love
I came to the crowd for understanding

I found you
I came to the crowd to weep
I came to the crowd to laugh

You dried my tears
You shared my happiness

I went from the crowd seeking you
I went from the crowd seeking me
I went from the crowd forever

You came, too

"*My father has always played some part in my life.*"

Kristin Lems

LIFE WITHOUT FATHER

● Divorce is never easy on anyone, but from the pain of separation can come new understanding. What children need to know, of course, is that whatever happens, their parents still love them.

OR A LONG TIME, AS LONG AS I CAN REMEMBER, my parents' divorce was a thing I could not touch because it was too near. I left its immediate hurt with training wheels and jump rope, but something within me still stung at the mention of the word *father*.

My father has always played some part in my life — the rugged disciplinarian, the successful man of business, or the occasional correspondent. After the divorce his role diminished steadily. Just as Darwin's evolutionary animals compensate for missing parts by growing new ones, I gradually replaced the blank spots with other men. Yet, Daddy was there. He existed in my obscure "second life" on weekends.

I am told now that when I was young, while crying, I asked my mother, "Doesn't Daddy like me?" This outburst was my response to all my years of contact with him: He never seemed to really like me. It was partly because I was female, and he looked on women as giddy, nonsensical, oversensitive, and generally scatterbrained. Because there was no place for serious discussion with a young girl, anything I said was immediately dismissed by his abrupt and disdainful comments. I often found myself in the position of not knowing who to be while with him — myself, or a giddy, mindless girl.

When he remarried, my sister and I were confronted with a strange woman not at all like my mother. She was amiably inarticulate, domestic, and fashionable. She possessed all the qualities Daddy seemed to think I lacked — levelheadedness, style, and subservience. I resented his new life because I was left out. He had no place for a clumsy and headstrong little girl who could only remind him of an unpleasant past.

My feelings of rejection were not all fantasy. One day my sister and I were visiting him at his home when a prospective business associate came by. The man did not know of Daddy's remarriage, and to make things all appear aboveboard, we were pulled aside and told to call our father "Uncle Bill."

Time passed and the family grew. My half-siblings were remote; each made me a little less important to my father. The distance between us, however, was most firmly secured when Daddy was transferred to Italy for four years. This move confirmed what I had already known: I had no influence on his life at all.

Four years is a long time to be without a father. Our relationship consisted only of letters, a circumstance that gave me a new chance to express myself honestly to him. It was somehow easier to speak sincerely when I didn't have to look into his unyielding eyes. It was during this period that I finally began to look objectively at my father and at our situation.

When the four years ended, last summer, his family and I vacationed together for two weeks — a sort of reacquaintance period. I watched after his children and had an opportunity to speak seriously to him with more success. I felt more like an independent young lady with valid ideas than a sullen daughter. And he seemed to feel my growth, too. He was willing, even glad, to explain the Italian government to me, for instance, or to discuss any other subject that interested me. I was making headway.

At the same time, I was forming friendships with my peer group on the lake. Summer and youth are somehow very conducive to romance; each summer I almost invariably got close to a boy. These friendships followed the course of most — very turbulant and short-lived. They created some tearful evenings for me, sleeping alone in our dark cottage. Early one morning I slipped inside the house and sat in the dark living room, silently weeping and bemoaning my young fate. I heard muted footsteps on the stairs. Someone was coming down to see me. There was surprise and joy in my heart as I saw my father, lighted by moonlight, descend the stairs in his bathrobe. He came and sat down close to me.

"I heard you down here and I thought I'd come and talk to you."

"Thank you," I said, hardly daring to breathe for fear of betraying my sobs.

"I know you're upset," he pushed on, knocking down those walls of superficiality that had kept us apart. "And how could I sleep, knowing my first daughter is upset?"

My heart beat wildly. First daughter! First born! He had said it with pride in his voice. He went on. "I know it's a hard thing, this growing business. I wish I could have been around through more of it. But now that I'm back, we'll get to know each other again."

And now I was crying for all I was worth, and it was for joy. A sentence was trembling within me: "I have a father! I have a father!" He sat up all night with me, losing his sleep, and slowly gaining back his daughter. He listened to me as he would listen to anyone; yet I was a special person, a daughter, his first born.

At last we climbed up to our bedrooms. His goodnight was so fatherly, I could hardly stand from trembling. I lay in bed shaking with joy at my discovery. I have a father. After sixteen years I have found a father.

A CLOSER LOOK

1. Did the girl's problems with her father exist before the divorce? What were these problems?

2. What other problems did the divorce and remarriage create for the daughter? Do you think these problems could have been avoided?

3. At the end of the story, the girl feels that she has found her father again. What would you advise them both to do to keep this new relationship growing?

• Often we judge our success in terms of our personal accomplishments on the athletic field and in the classroom. But perhaps we also ought to measure success in terms of the things we share with other people.

Mari Evans

IF THERE BE SORROW

If there be sorrow
let it be
for things undone
undreamed
    unrealized
        unattained

to these add one:
love withheld
    restrained.

"And remember, there is nothing you can't do."

Alice Steinbach

CALVIN: A BOY OF UNUSUAL VISION

● Each of us must face some difficulties in life. Steinbach won a 1985 Pulitzer Prize in Journalism for this article about a blind boy named Calvin and his triumph over his handicap. His secret? A courageous spirit — and the love of the people around him.

FIRST, THE EYES: THEY ARE LARGE AND BLUE, A light, opaque[1] blue, the color of a robin's egg. And if, on a sunny spring day, you look straight into these eyes — eyes that cannot look back at you — the sharp, April light turns them pale, like the thin blue of a high, cloudless sky.

Ten-year-old Calvin Stanley, the owner of these eyes and a boy who has been blind since birth, likes this description and asks to hear it twice. He listens as only he can listen, then: "Orange used to be my favorite color but now it's blue," he announces. Pause. The eyes flutter between the short, thick lashes. "I know there's light blue and there's dark blue, but what does sky-blue look like?" he wants to know. And if you watch his face as he listens to your description, you get a sense of a picture being clicked firmly into place behind the pale eyes.

He is a boy who has a lot of pictures stored in his head, retrievable images which have been fashioned for him by the people who love him — by family and friends and teachers who have painstakingly and patiently gone about creating a special world for

Calvin's inner eye to inhabit.

"Child," his mother once told him, "one day I won't be here and I won't be around to pick you up — so you have to try to be something on your own. You have to learn how to deal with this. And to do that, you have to learn how to think."

Calvin's mother: "When Calvin was little, he was so inquisitive. He wanted to see everything, he wanted to touch everything. I had to show him every little thing there is. A spoon, a fork. I let him play with them, just hold them. The pots, the pans. *Everything.* I showed him the sharp edges of the table. 'You cannot touch this; it will hurt you.' And I showed him what would hurt. He still bumped into it anyway, but he knew what he wasn't supposed to do and what he could do. And he knew that nothing in his room — *nothing* could hurt him.

"And when he started walking and we went out together — I guess he was about two — I never said anything to him about what to do. When we got to the curbs, Calvin knew that when I stopped, he should step down, and when I stopped again, he should step up. I never said anything, that's just the way we did it. And it became a pattern."

Calvin remembers when he began to realize that something about him was "different": "I just figured it out myself. I think I was about four. I would pick things up and I couldn't see them. Other people would say they could see things and I couldn't."

And his mother remembers the day her son asked her why he was blind and other people weren't.

"He must have been about four or five. I explained to him what happened, that he was born that way and that it was nobody's fault and he didn't have to blame himself. He asked, 'Why me?' And I said, 'I don't know why, Calvin. Maybe there's a special plan for you in your life and there's a reason for this. But this is the way you're going to be and you can deal with it.' "

Then she sat her son down and told him this: "You're *seeing,* Calvin. You're just using your hands instead of your eyes. But you're seeing. And remember, there is *nothing* you can't do."

It's spring vacation and Calvin is out in the alley behind his house riding his bike, a serious-looking, black and silver two-wheeler. "Stay behind me," he shouts to his friend Kellie Bass, who's furiously pedaling her bike down the one-block stretch of alley

"You have to learn how to deal with this."

where Calvin is allowed to bicycle.

Now: Try to imagine riding a bike without being able to see where you're going. Without even knowing what an "alley" looks like. Try to imagine how you navigate a space that has no visual boundaries, that exists only in your head. And then try to imagine what Calvin is feeling as he pedals his bike in that space, whooping for joy as the air rushes past him on either side.

And although Calvin can't see the signs of spring sprouting all around him in the neighboring backyards — the porch furniture and barbecue equipment being brought out of storage, the grass growing emerald green from the April rains, the forsythia exploding yellow over the fences — still, there are signs of another sort which guide him along his route:

Past the German shepherd who always barks at him, telling Calvin that he's three houses away from his home; then past the purple hyacinths, five gardens away, throwing out their fragrance (later it will be the scent of the lilacs which guides him); past the large diagonal crack which lifts the front wheel of his bike up and then down, telling him he's reached his boundary and should turn back — past all these familiar signs Calvin rides his bike on a warm spring day.

There's a baseball game about to start in Calvin's backyard, and Mrs. Stanley is pitching to her son. Nine-year-old Kellie, on first base, has taken off her fake fur coat so she can get a little more steam into her game; and the other team member, Monet Clark, six, is catching. It is also Monet's job to alert Calvin, who's at bat, when to swing. "Hit it, Calvin," she yells. "Swing!"

He does, and the sound of the ball making solid contact with the bat sends Calvin running off to first base, his hands groping in front of his body. His mother walks over to stand next to him at first base and unconsciously her hands go to his head, stroking his hair in a soft, protective movement.

"Remember," the mother had said to her son six years earlier, "there's *nothing* you can't do."

Calvin's father, thirty-seven-year-old Calvin Stanley, Jr., a Baltimore city policeman, has taught his son how to ride a bike and how to shift gears in the family's Volkswagen and how to put toys together.

The father: "You know, there's nothing much I've missed with him. Because he does everything. Except see. He goes swimming out in the pool in the backyard. Some of the other kids are afraid of the water, but he jumps right in, puts his head under. If it were me I wouldn't be as brave as he is. I probably wouldn't go anywhere. If it were me I'd probably stay in this house most of the time. But he's always ready to go, always on the telephone, ready to do something.

"But he gets sad, too. You can just look at him sometimes and tell he's real sad."

The son: "You know what makes me sad? *Charlotte's Web*. It's my favorite story. I listen to the record at night. I like Charlotte, the spider. The way she talks. And, you know, she really loved Wilbur, the pig. He was her best friend." Calvin's voice is full of warmth and wonder as he talks about E. B. White's tale of the spider who befriended a pig and later sacrificed herself for him.

"It's a story about friendship. It's telling us how good friends are supposed to be. Like Charlotte and Wilbur," he says, turning away from you suddenly to wipe his eyes. "And when Charlotte dies, it makes me real sad. I always feel like I've lost a friend. That's why I try not to listen to that part. I just move the needle forward."

Something else makes Calvin sad: "I'd like to see what my mother looks like," he says, looking up quickly and swallowing hard. "What does she look like? People tell me she's pretty."

The mother: "One day Calvin wanted me to tell him how I looked. He was about six. They were doing something in school for Mother's Day and the kids were drawing pictures of their mothers. So I took his hand. I tried to explain about skin — let him touch his, and then mine.

"And I think that was the moment when Calvin really *knew* he was blind, because he said, 'I won't ever be able to see your face . . . or Daddy's face,'" she says softly, covering her eyes with her hands, but not in time to stop the tears. "That's the only time I've ever let it bother me that much."

But Mrs. Stanley knew what to tell her only child: "I said, 'Calvin, you *can* see my face. You can see it with your hands and by listening to my voice, and you can tell more about me that way than somebody who can use his eyes.' "

Thirty-three-year-old Ethel Stanley, a handsome, strong-looking woman with a radiant smile, is the oldest of seven children and grew up looking after her younger brothers and sisters while her mother worked. "She was a wonderful mother," Mrs. Stanley recalls. "Yes, she had to work, but when she was there, she was with you every minute and those minutes were worth a whole day. She always had time to listen to you."

Somewhere — perhaps from her own childhood experiences — Mrs. Stanley, who has not worked since Calvin was born, acquired the ability to nurture[2] and teach and poured her mothering love into Calvin. And it shows. He moves in the sighted world with trust and faith and the unshakable confidence of a child whose mother has always been there for him. "If you don't understand something, ask," she tells Calvin again and again, in her open, forthright way. "Just ask."

"When he was little he wanted to be Stevie Wonder," says Calvin's father, laughing. "He started playing the piano and he got pretty good at it. Now he wants to be a computer programmer and design programs for the blind."

Calvin's neatly ordered bedroom is outfitted with all the comforts you would find in the room of many ten-year-old, middle-class boys: a television set (black and white, he tells you), an Atari game with a box of cartridges (his favorite is "Phoenix"), a braille Monopoly

41

"He does everything. Except see."

set, records, tapes, and programmed talking robots. "I watch wrestling on TV every Saturday," he says. "I wrestle with my friends. It's fun."

He moves around his room confidently and easily. "I know this house like a book." Still, some things are hard for him to remember since, in his case, much of what he remembers has to be imagined visually first, like the size and color of his room. "I think it's kind of big," he says of the small room. "And it's green," he says of the deep rose-colored walls.

And while Calvin doesn't need to turn the light on in his room, he does like to have some kind of sound going constantly. *Loud* sound.

"It's three o'clock," he says, as the theme music from a TV show blares out into his room.

"Turn that TV down," says his mother evenly. "You're not *deaf*, you know."

It's two p.m. in Vivian Jackson's class, Room 207.

What Calvin can't see: He can't see the small, pretty girl sitting opposite him, the one who is wearing little rows of red, yellow, and blue barrettes shaped like airplanes in her braided hair. He can't see the line of small, green plants growing in yellow pots all along the sunny window sill. And he can't see Mrs. Jackson in her rose-pink suit and pink enameled earrings shaped like little swans.

("Were they really shaped like little swans?" he will ask later.)

But Calvin can feel the warm spring breeze — invisible to *everyone's* eyes, not just his — blowing in through the window, and he can hear the tapping of a young oak tree's branches against the window. He can hear Mrs. Jackson's pleasant, musical voice and, later, if you ask him what she looks like, he will say, "She's nice."

But best of all, Calvin can read and spell and do fractions and follow the classroom work in his specially prepared braille books. He is smart and he can do everything the rest of his class can do. Except see.

"What's the next word, Calvin?" Mrs. Jackson asks.

"Eleven," he says, reading from his braille textbook.

"Now tell us how to spell it — without looking back at the book!" she says quickly, causing Calvin's fingers to fly away from the forbidden word.

"E-l-e-v-e-n," he spells out easily.

An important part of Calvin's school experience has been his contact with sighted children.

"When he first started school," his mother recalls, "some of the kids would tease him about his eyes. 'Oh, they're so big and you can't see.' But I just told him, 'Not any time in your life will everybody around you like you — whether you can see or not. They're just children and they don't know they're being cruel. And I'm sure it's not the last time someone will be cruel to you. But it's all up to you because you have to go to school and you'll have to deal with it.' "

Calvin's teachers say he's well liked, and watching him on the playground and in class you get the impression that the only thing that singles him out from the other kids is that someone in his class is always there to take his hand if he needs help.

"I'd say he's really well accepted," says his mobility teacher, Miss Dyer, "and that he's got a couple of very special friends."

Eight-year-old Brian Butler is one of these special friends. "My *best* friend," says Calvin proudly, introducing you to a studious-looking boy whose eyes are alert and serious behind his glasses. The two boys are not in the same class, but they ride home together on the bus every day.

Here's Brian explaining why he likes Calvin so much: "He's funny and he makes me laugh. And I like him because he always makes me feel better when I don't feel good." And, he says, his friendship with Calvin is no different from any other good friendship. Except for one thing: "If Calvin's going to bump into a wall or something, I tell him, 'Look out,' " says Brian, sounding as though it were the most natural thing in the world to do when walking with a friend.

"Charlotte would have done it for Wilbur," is the way Calvin sizes up Brian's help, evoking once more that story about "how friendship ought to be."

[1] **opaque:** not allowing entrance or passage of light
[2] **nurture:** nourish; train

A CLOSER LOOK

1. What has Calvin's mother done to help her son? What other people have helped him? What did they do, and why did they do it?

2. Describe Calvin's personality. How has his personality helped him to deal with his handicap?

3. If you were blind, what do you think would be the greatest challenge for you to deal with?

Erma Bombeck

YOU DON'T LOVE ME

• Loving parents are not people who say yes to everything their children ask for — at least not according to the popular newspaper columnist Erma Bombeck. Loving parents sometimes must say no if they are to help their children to become strong and independent, and able to survive on their own. Bombeck's tone is ironical and humorous, but the message underneath is full of tenderness and love.

"**Y**OU DON'T LOVE ME!" HOW MANY TIMES have your kids laid that one on you? And how many times have you, as a parent, resisted the urge to tell them how much? Someday, when my children are old enough to understand the logic that motivates a mother, I'll tell them:

I loved you enough to bug you about where you were going, and with whom, and what time you would get home.

I loved you enough to insist you buy a bike with your own money that we could afford and you couldn't.

I loved you enough to be silent and let you discover your hand-picked friend was a creep.

I loved you enough to make you return a Milky Way with a bite out of it to a drugstore and confess, "I stole this."

I loved you enough to stand over you for two hours while you cleaned your bedroom, a job that would have taken me fifteen minutes.

"I loved you enough to accept you for what you are."

I loved you enough to say, "Yes, you can go to Disney World on Mother's Day."

I loved you enough to let you see anger, disappointment, disgust, and tears in my eyes.

I loved you enough not to make excuses for your lack of respect and your bad manners.

I loved you enough to admit that I was wrong and ask your forgiveness.

I loved you enough to ignore "what every other mother" did or said.

I loved you enough to let you stumble, fall, hurt, and fail.

I loved you enough to let you assume the responsibility for your own actions, at six, ten, or sixteen.

I loved you enough to figure you would lie about the party being chaperoned, but forgave you for it . . . after discovering I was right.

I loved you enough to shove you off my lap, let go of your hand, be mute to your pleas . . . so that you had to stand alone.

I loved you enough to accept you for what you are, not what I wanted you to be.

But most of all, I loved you enough to say no when you hated me for it. That was the hardest part of all.

A CLOSER LOOK

1. Each sentence that starts "I loved you enough" refers to a particular incident. Which of these incidents made the child upset at the time? Which of them hurt the mother at the time?

2. What kinds of things do most people do to show their love? Why are Bombeck's actions unusual ways to show love? How would she define love?

3. What is Erma Bombeck trying to tell us about a parent's role in the development of his or her children?

● Gary Soto, one of America's best-known Chicano poets, brings to life an evening from the years when he was growing up. In this poem, he describes the pride and happiness that result from a generous act.

Gary Soto

ORANGES

The first time I walked
With a girl, I was twelve,
Cold, and weighted down
With two oranges in my jacket.
December. Frost cracking
Beneath my steps, my breath
Before me, then gone,
As I walked toward
Her house, the one whose
Porch light burned yellow
Night and day, in any weather.
A dog barked at me, until
She came out pulling
At her gloves, face bright
With rouge. I smiled,
Touched her shoulder, and led
Her down the street, across
A used car lot and a line
Of newly planted trees,
Until we were breathing
Before a drugstore. We
Entered, the tiny bell
Bringing a saleslady
Down a narrow aisle of goods.
I turned to the candies
Tiered like bleachers,
And asked what she wanted —

Light in her eyes, a smile
Starting at the corners
Of her mouth. I fingered
A nickel in my pocket,
And when she lifted a chocolate
That cost a dime,
I didn't say anything.
I took the nickel from
My pocket, then an orange,
And set them quietly on
The counter. When I looked up,
The lady's eyes met mine,
And held them, knowing
Very well what it was all
About.

                    Outside,
A few cars hissing past,
Fog hanging like old
Coats between the trees.
I took my girl's hand
In mine for two blocks,
Then released it to let
Her unwrap the chocolate.
I peeled my orange
That was so bright against
The gray of December
That, from some distance,
Someone might have thought
I was making a fire in my hands.

"We'd crowd around, joshing him, spinning his chair."

Norman Rosten

JUMPY

• This is a story about a boy with special problems and special friends. That good intentions can cause pain to others doesn't seem fair, but perhaps it's better to have good intentions than not to try to help at all.

O F ALL THE PEOPLE WHO MOVED INTO OUR house, I guess I remember Philip the best. He was older than I, about fourteen, sad-eyed, skinny, and had to spend most of the time in a wheelchair. He had something we'd never heard of before on our block: an enlarged heart. Pretty soon we called him Jumpy because his heart could be seen jumping right under his skin when his shirt was open. The spot on his chest would go *poom-boom poom-boom* (without a sound) up and down, no bigger than a dime. It was weird. Yet after a while we got used to it. Watching it was like a game.

When Jumpy was wheeled out in his chair on the sidewalk to sit in the morning sun, he'd wave his arm and call, "It's me, fellas." And we'd crowd around, joshing him, spinning his chair, until someone would say, "Let's see it jump, how about it, Jumpy!" And grinning shyly, he opened his shirt, as we stared at the pulsing circle of flesh — his real, alive heart!

Jumpy smiled feebly. "The doctor says I'll get better. I might even go back to school after summer vacation." We said nothing.

We didn't know much about hearts, but it didn't look as though he would be in school for a long time.

I would stop into his room almost every day. He sat up in bed, reading or listening to the radio, or just leaning back looking into space. I would sometimes come in and he wouldn't see me. The room was so silent I'd think he was dead. I'd call out, "Jumpy?" And he would turn slowly, his eyes brightening. "Hi, sit down."

We talked about all kinds of things. Baseball and horses and radios. He had a small crystal set. We wondered how music came from an inch of wire probing a piece of crystal — with no electricity! We talked about school, science, and the tutor who came to the house. That was before he got too sick and stopped studying altogether. We played cards a lot.

His mother was nice, but sad, as if she knew something was going to happen. She brought us cakes and ice cream while we played our games. They had to be quiet games because he couldn't get excited; that made it worse, his mother explained.

Sometimes my sister would visit. She was shy, and she usually brought him some little gift, like a jelly-apple or a bag of cherries. He loved cherries.

"You look better, Philip," my sister said on these visits. (She never called him Jumpy; she used his real name.)

"Thank you," Jumpy replied.

"You look much better than last week, honest, Philip," she said. And he smiled his thin but intense smile. He never said much to her. She, as well, was embarrassed. She was shy all the time. I was conscious of her growing up, and it made me feel a little strange. I found myself watching her. I saw her sleeping once, but I didn't hang around — I was just getting something from the room. Anyway, her growing up and Jumpy's growing up made them shy with each other. I thought he liked her, but I wasn't sure about what she felt.

Once, when we were talking about girls, Jumpy said he thought my sister was a nice kid.

"Did you ever kiss a girl?" I asked him.

"No. Did you?"

"Yes," I said.

"I don't mean sisters," he said.

I had, in fact, earlier that summer, kissed a slender, light-haired girl good night. It wasn't much of a kiss, but I recalled the warmth of her lips with a shiver. It was quick; in the movies they were long kisses, but I suppose that was for older people. Anyway, standing on the stoop was bad for your balance, and that slender girl and I just brushed faces, you might say. Still, I wasn't lying when I said I had kissed a girl.

"What was it like?" he wanted to know.

I scratched my head and gulped one of the cherries. "It was like . . . very different. I wouldn't know how to describe it, Jumpy. All I can say is, I'd do it again if I got the chance."

"I'd sure like to try it," said Jumpy. "But I guess you gotta ask a girl. They just won't come over and kiss you, would they?"

I shook my head. "I don't think so. I never heard of it. Maybe if it was something special they would."

"Well, anyway . . . " Jumpy's voice trailed off. "It isn't going to happen to me, I guess." We continued to play cards.

Later, alone with her, I asked my sister, "What do you think about Jumpy?"

"You mean Philip? I hate that nickname. He's too nice to have such a nickname."

"Do you like him?"

"Oh, he's all right." She looked at me curiously. "Why?"

"Nothing. Only he asks about you a lot. He's goofy about you."

She simpered. "You know what you are? You're absolutely cuckoo," she said.

I shot back at her, "He'd love to smooch with you. He keeps saying he'd *love* to kiss you. What about *that*?"

"I am not interested in kissing Philip," she said imperiously.[1] But underneath I knew the idea scared her. After all, she was just a kid, and she was growing up and thinking about things like kissing. I was. And so was everybody else, I figured.

I kept thinking of Jumpy, in bed most of the time, with a doctor coming by twice a week, and not once being kissed by a girl. When I thought of all the kissing going on on the beach, and under the boardwalk, and practically everywhere — well, it was a shame about Jumpy.

He took a turn for the worse. He wasn't out of the house for days. His mother wouldn't allow any of us to come into his room. Once I peeked in and saw him lying on the bed, his head turned toward the wall. I called out softly, "Hey, Jumpy." He moved his head, lifted his arm weakly, but didn't turn. I went away. That night, the doctor arrived on a special visit. My mother met him in the hall and went inside the room with him. I tried to enter, but they wouldn't let me. I listened at the door. All I could hear were muffled voices and, I thought, a sound of weeping.

The next day, when I asked my mother what happened, she only said, "He's very sick," and went about her work. I waited in the hall until Jumpy's mother came out of the room. When she saw me, she said in a whisper, "My poor little boy." She pressed my hand and went off into the street.

I pushed the door open into Jumpy's room. He was alone. I went up to the bed. I hadn't seen him for over a week, and I was shocked. His face seemed to be stretched thin like paper; the eyes had sunken deep into their sockets; the mouth was thin and blue. His pajama shirt was open, and I could see his heart leaping against his skin. In my ears it suddenly sounded *poom-boom poom-boom*, louder and louder. I swallowed and the sound went away.

Jumpy saw me. "Boy, I must be sick with doctors coming around every day."

"You look OK," I lied.

"I don't know, I broke the mirror yesterday lookin'," he said, with that odd persisting smile playing around his mouth. "I must look like some kind of freaky ghost."

I didn't know what to say, because he was right. I pushed his shoulder jokingly. He sighed, leaned back on the pillow, and stared at the ceiling. "Jimmy and the guys send their regards," I said hesitatingly.

He said, "I had a dream about Jimmy. You'll never guess what it was. You won't tell him?" I shook my head. "I mean, he might think I had something against him."

"What'd you dream?" I prodded him.

"You won't laugh? I dreamed he was dead." He started to laugh, and I laughed, and we both laughed so loud I thought we'd both get a stomachache. Jumpy started to cough, and I rushed to get him some water. He choked on the water and I had to slap him on the back. Then we got to talking about some other things. Baseball. The law of gravity. And, again, girls. He asked about my sister again; she hadn't been in to say hello for over a week. I mumbled some apology for her and after a while I left.

I met my sister outside. She was sitting in the sun reading a book. "I saw Jumpy just now — I mean Philip. He asked about you."

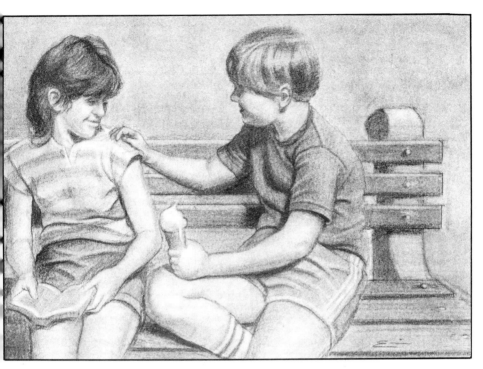

"Just kiss him. Just once. Would you please?"

She continued reading. "I was wondering, Sis . . . would you go up and say hello? He's pretty sick."

"I might later on. I'm reading now, can't you see?"

"When you go up, would you do me a favor? Don't get mad. Would you kiss him?" She stopped her reading. Her eyes widened. "Just kiss him. Just once. Would you please?"

"Why should I?"

"Well, he's awful sick — but it's not catching like a cold or anything. He's so blue. You'd cheer him up. Would you?"

She snapped her book shut and rose. "Please leave me alone or I'll tell Momma." And she ran into the house.

Not many days later, Jumpy's mother came over to me on the street, her eyes numb. "He's dying. Any day now, the doctor says. We mustn't feel bad. It's best with such a disease."

All that afternoon in my ear, even when I swallowed, was the sound *poom-boom poom-boom,* and any minute that heart might stop!

I spoke to my sister again, as she was leaving the kitchen after dinner.

"He asked for you again."

She was skeptical. "You're making it up."

"No," I pleaded. "He's awfully lonely. If you'd see him for a minute, that's all, and just kiss him — "

"If you don't stop that — " She turned to go.

I gripped her arm. "Don't be a stuck-up. If a friend asks you for a kiss, is that a crime?"

"I don't like him."

"Do you have to like a fella, I mean a friend, to kiss him, just one kiss!"

She broke away and ran to my mother, sobbing. "I won't do it. He wants me to kiss Philip. I won't, I won't."

My mother, startled, comforted her. "Quiet, you don't have to kiss anyone if you don't want to." She turned to me. "What is it now?"

I kept my eyes lowered. I didn't know how to explain such a thing. "I just asked her to kiss Jumpy. What's so terrible about it?" I was getting sore at my sister. "Anyway, she's a stuck-up!" I ran to the street, sullen, furious, defeated.

At bedtime, my sister came to my room. I could see she had come to be forgiven. Standing at the door, she said, "I'm sorry I told Momma on you. That was wrong." I didn't answer. I'd gotten too tired thinking of Jumpy and his heart that would stop any minute.

She didn't go. "I hope you're not mad," she said. "After all, I don't know Philip, not really, I mean . . . "

Her voice trailed off in uncertainty.

"If you do it, I'll give you a dollar. I promise. Gosh, how can you say you don't know him?" She was silent. "It ain't so awful kissing someone. You've kissed me lots of times."

"Kissing you is not the same, and you know it," she replied, wavering.

"It can't be much different with Jimmy. He's my age, about."

"The whole thing is silly, but I'll do it." Her acceptance, finally, was so casual, I couldn't understand all the fuss she had made earlier. What a screwloose for a sister, I thought! "When do I do it?" she asked.

"Right now," I said. She looked calm, as though she kissed boys every day, which I don't think she did, but it crossed my mind. I didn't see her much during the day. "Come on," I said. She followed me down the hallway. We came to his door. I knocked softly. We entered. He was alone, his eyes half-closed. I thought he was asleep until he spoke.

"Hello. I'm glad you came." His eyes, now fully opened, rested on my sister. She walked to the bed, her walk light, almost jaunty. "Hi, Philip. I'm sorry I haven't been up to see you lately. But you look fine."

He smiled weakly. His face was yellowed. He opened his mouth but his voice was so low I had to lean over to hear him. "Good night," he said.

"Sure, Jumpy, we won't stay." I turned to my sister and nodded to her. "We just dropped in for a quick hello. See you again tomorrow."

"Tomorrow," he whispered. His fingers reached over but could barely grip my hand.

"See you again," said my sister. She leaned over the bed, her eyes tightly shut, her face moving close to his. With a cry, he turned his head into the pillow. My sister looked at me, her lips trembling, and fled from the room. "Get out," Jumpy shouted. "Leave me alone. I don't want to see anybody!" I backed slowly toward the door, stunned by his anger.

The next afternoon, it was hard for me to imagine it was him in the coffin. I thought of his small heart quiet now under his clean shirt, and the *poom-boom* in my ear was quiet, too.

My sister cried a little. She was mad at me for a long time, for months, and wouldn't talk to me. Sometimes she'd lose her temper and scream at me even when I didn't remember doing anything wrong.

¹ **imperiously:** in an arrogant and domineering manner

A CLOSER LOOK

1. What is Philip's (Jumpy's) physical problem?

2. What does the narrator of this story try to do to help Jumpy? Why does he think this will help?

3. How do you think the narrator felt after Jumpy died? How would you have felt? Why?

"Mike always spoke in a distant, wonderful way."

Jim Tolley

CLIMBING THE DAYMARKER

● Some of your most difficult and challenging relationships are with your brothers and sisters. As you grow up together, you may compete, fight, and share with one another; you may be best friends one day and bitter rivals the next. The relationships between brothers and sisters constantly change, but they last a lifetime.

LOOKING BACK, MOST THINGS GROW SMALL WITH years. On the island where I spent my summers as a child, the wharves no longer reach far over the sea, and the saltbox cottage where my family lived appears to me gray and simple.

Alone among the objects of my memory, the daymarker stands as tall as ever. Built long before the lighthouse, it stood at the crest of the dunes to guide the lobster boats into the harbor. The marker rose as high as our house. It was built of four thick poles slanted together at the top, like a pyramid. Nailed across on the sides were wooden slats that led up like the rungs on a ladder.

Until I was ten years old, our last summer on the island, I had never climbed the daymarker. The poles, worn smooth by blowing sands, had no handholds, and I was too small to reach the lowest slat. Up to then, the top of the daymarker belonged to my brother Mike. When that changed we both changed with it.

Mike had always been a sort of mentor[1] to me. I would awaken in the early morning, peek from the bunk bed at my brother below, and

59

gently shake the bed until he woke, too. Then I would ask, "What will we do today?" Whatever he said, we would do. Most days we spent catching crabs with squid bait at the marina, or pulling sea urchins from the boat ramp. My favorite game was to take a handful of hermit crabs and set them out on the sand and wait for them to crawl from their borrowed shells. We always ended the day by heading, after dinner, to the dunes, following our private trail through the sawgrass. There Mike would climb the daymarker. While I sat in the cooling sand, he would tell me what he could see from the top. Each evening there would be something new to report, a different trawler in the harbor or a freighter pressing the cape. From his spot at the top of the daymarker, Mike always spoke in a distant, wonderful way, a way in which I had never spoken.

When I turned ten, I stopped waking Mike in the morning. I felt a need to be out alone. One morning I found a dead ray on the beach, and another time I picked up the brittle black egg of a mermaid's purse. When I told my parents of these things at dinner, Mike would pretend not to listen. Then he would head out, as always, to the daymarker. I didn't want to follow.

Near the end of the season an old woman who painted watercolors on an easel in front of her cottage saw me carrying a horseshoe crab and asked me to pose. I held the crab out like a trophy. As she painted, the old woman asked me where my brother was; she had seen us on the beach together early that summer. I told her that I didn't know. When she finished, I ran home late for dinner. Mother had kept my food warm. I gulped it down, then ran out to tell Mike about the portrait. Mike was atop the pyramid, but didn't look at me when I told the story. He didn't say a thing, and would not say what he saw from the peak. What was he seeing? I kicked around in the sand for a while, then left him alone.

The next day I was down at the marina when I saw something bigger than a crab moving beneath a moored sailboat. I walked across the dock for a closer look. It was a lobster. I stripped off my shirt and sneakers, dove in, grabbed the lobster, and pulled it out. I took it home, and we boiled it for dinner. Since I had brought home the main course, Mother had Mike wash the dishes even though it was my turn. I ran out to the dunes, happy and not really thinking of Mike back in the house.

The daymarker looked very tall, without anyone on top. There was no one around, and I decided to climb it if I could. I had never really tried, not that year; and when I jumped up I was surprised to grab the first slat with ease. I swung a leg over and pulled myself up. The whitewash on the wood rubbed off onto my legs and arms. I was new to this, not like my brother who climbed it cleanly. The height made me feel euphoric,[2] even though the wood slivered my hands. When I reached the peak, I steadied myself and sat. The sun was setting behind me. The sea and sky were fading, but as sharp and clear as anything I had ever seen. I looked over the water at the last sailboats heading in, and at the lighthouse as the turning beam switched on.

"What — " I heard Mike below. I looked down and saw him climbing up, climbing after me. For an instant I was startled, not understanding his anger. I started to say, "I would've asked!" but I could see that it didn't matter. Mike was still bigger than I was. I tried to keep him away with my feet, but he grabbed my ankle and twisted until I began to lose my grip. I kicked, but he was too strong. He pulled on my leg, prying me from the top slat, until I fell.

I tumbled face down and couldn't breathe until I cleared the sand from my face. I spit the sand from my mouth and felt where I had cut my lip. I wiped the blood with my arm as I knelt, then stood up and looked at my brother. He was seated at the top, looking east over the water as if nothing had happened between us.

I could've climbed back up and fought him, but the top of the daymarker wasn't so important anymore. When I think about it, I remember the way the cut on my lip healed very slowly. The taste of blood, like rust, seeped for weeks into my mouth. When I remember the day, I realize I had seen more from the daymarker's base, thrown down, than I could ever have seen from its top.

[1] **mentor:** trusted advisor or guide
[2] **euphoric:** state of feeling great joy

A CLOSER LOOK

1. How old are the two brothers in this story? What was their relationship in the past? How does it change during the summer?

2. Why do you think Mike climbs the daymarker? Why do you think his younger brother tries to climb it? How does Mike react? Why?

3. Which brother do you sympathize with? Why?

● Every family is different from every other family, each with its own customs, values, and memories. In this poem, Tina shares with you her memories of her grandmother. Although the details are special, the warm feeling of belonging to a family is common to us all.

Tina Pomeroy

MAKING POTICA

— for Leopoldina, Johana, and me

We sit in Gramma's kitchen,
warmed by the oven,
our fingers aching from cracking nuts
for the potica.

We watch Gramma
as she takes off her ring,
sets it on the windowsill
next to her birthday fern.
The bread swell of her belly
tucked under an apron,
she rolls up her sleeves,
arms showing round and white
like the dough she begins to knead
between her fingers.

Against the table
she slaps and smacks the dough,
folds it in on itself
again and again.

Flour rises in storms,
clouds around her face.
Her body knows the rhythm
of this bread
as the peach trees of Rijeka[1]
know the seasons.

Gramma rolls the dough thin,
ladles out the thick swell
of cellar honey, spreads it smooth.
She sows the nuts like seeds,
sprinkles on the sweet *rayene*
dried from the grapes
whose vines tangle across the back porch.

"*Yez patee
ba gzita Nomaraila*,"
she sings and winks to us.
But we don't understand
those words she couldn't leave
in Belgrade.[1]
We only know the song of the dough,
the music she makes with her hands.

[1] **Rijeka, Belgrade:** cities in Yugoslavia

"I am alone, too."

Julie Lochnicht

GROWING OLDER

● As you grow older, your relationships with other members of
your family may change, especially your relationships with your
parents. Sometimes it even seems that they have become different
people over the years — or is it you who are different now?

A S HE SITS AND WATCHES THE BALL GAME, HE
cheers and yells. I sit beside him, and cheer and yell, too.
I don't know what's going on, but I'm with him; we're
together doing the same thing.

Sometimes I just like to look at him reading the paper or telling a
joke at the dinner table. I ask my mother, "Do you think I take after
Dad?" A small grin comes over her face, and I hear, "Oh, yes,
dear. You and your father have a lot in common."

"Am I funny like him, too?"

"Oh, yes."

I skip out of the kitchen into the living room and sit next to him
on the couch. He kisses me, squeezes me tightly for a long time,
then swings me up on his shoulders and carries me to bed.

"I love you, Daddy. I love you a lot."

When I lie in my bed, I picture him in my mind. How big and
strong he is. When I get older I'm going to be just like him. He
never really says he loves me but I know he does. I can feel it when
he holds me.

65

I was a little girl then, full of dreams made up of fairy tales, rainbows, and silver raindrops that held the magic touch of happiness. My father made me want to sing and dance, and I would, for him. Solos for an audience of one. Applause, applause. I was a princess and he was the king.

But that was a long time ago. Time has made me older, made me see more but know less. In a sad sense, it has made me wiser.

I was so sure time could never affect my father — or me. He would always be the same strong, happy person that I loved so much. But growing older has taken the gold and silver from my eyes, and now I see that his are not wondrous blue, but a faded, tired gray. The jokes he tells, the same ones he's always told, are no longer funny. They do not make me laugh. They are sad, mocking jokes of people and of life. When he puts his arm around me, its weight is heavy on my shoulder. When he takes my hand, his hold is too tight, too clasping.

My beautiful dad! I cannot see him as I did and I cannot accept him as I see him now. The words I had so easily spoken to him once are now too hard to say, the words of love.

Some nights, late, I see him in the darkened living room, just sitting, doing nothing, the clock ticking. I am alone, too. There are no such things as fairy princesses and kings, and the twinkling lights in the sky at night do not make wishes come true.

There were many children in my father's house. They were born, grew older, and went away. Only two of us are still at home. I think more about my brothers and sisters now than I did when they were here. I wonder who my father was for each of them. Did they know someone I never did? Did they understand him more? Did they love him better?

I watch my little brother often now. In his blue eyes there is love, contentment, fearlessness. He trusts easily.

I have asked him, "What is Father? Who is he?"

"Dad's big and strong!" he says. "He can do anything. Dad's going to build a ship," he says. "We're going to sail around the world. Dad tells me jokes and makes me laugh," he says. "I'm going to grow older and be just like him."

As he sits next to me, I hug him hard and try to squeeze some of his happiness into myself. I think for a while about what he has said, and I decide that, in this place, at this time, he knows his father in a more real way than he ever will again; so I play games with him and tell stories to him that have happy endings.

A CLOSER LOOK

1. *What was the narrator's image of her father when she was young? What is it now? What is her little brother's image of their dad?*

2. *Which of these many images does the narrator think is the "real" one? Why do you think she came to this conclusion?*

3. *Why do children tend to adore their parents when they are little? What other adults might they also adore?*

"Did parents worry about the figures their children cut?"

Jessamyn West

ROAD TO THE ISLES

● Have you ever worried that your parents would embarrass you? Cress Delahanty worries that her father will make a fool of himself in front of her best friend, Bernadine. What she discovers, however, is that parents worry about the impression their children make, too.

EVERYONE IS CONTINUALLY MAKING DISCOVERIES about himself and about other people. Sometimes these discoveries can come as a shock. On the night of the dance festival, Cress made some important discoveries.

It was the last Thursday in January, about nine in the evening, cold and raining. The three Delahantys sat close about the living-room fireplace — Mr. Delahanty at the built-in desk working on his schedule, Mrs. Delahanty on the sofa reading, and between them, crosswise in the wing chair, their fourteen-year-old daughter, Crescent. Cress was apparently studying the program of the folk-dance festival in which she was to appear the next evening. For the most part, however, she did not even see the program. She saw, instead, herself, infinitely graceful, moving through the figures of the dance that had been so difficult for her to master.

The high school folk-dancing class was made up of two kinds of performers — those with natural ability, who had themselves chosen the class, and those who, in the language of the physical education department, were "remedials." The remedials had been sent into the class willy-nilly in an effort to counteract in them defects ranging from antisocial attitudes to what Miss Ingols, the gym teacher, called "a general lack of grace." Cress had achieved the class under this final classification but now, at midterm, had so far outgrown it as to be the only remedial with a part in the festival.

The first five numbers on the program, "Tsiganotchka," "Ladies' Whim," "Meitschi Putz Di," "Hiawatha," and "Little Man in a Fix," Cress ignored. It was not only that she was not in these but that they were in no way as beautiful as "Road to the Isles," in which Mary Lou Hawkins, Chrystal O'Conor, Zelma Mayberry, Bernadine Deevers, and Crescent Delahanty took part. The mere sight of her name beside that of Bernadine Deevers, Tenant High School's most gifted dancer — most gifted *person*, really — instantly called up to Cress a vision of herself dancing not only the outward steps of "Road to the Isles" but its inner meaning: what Miss Ingols had called "the achievement of the impossible."

Cress thought that she was particularly adapted to dancing that meaning because she had so recently come that way herself. If she had been given three wishes when school opened in September, two of them would have been that Bernadine be her friend and that she herself succeed in the folk-dancing class. Both had then seemed equally impossible. Now not only did she have a part in the festival but Bernadine was her dear friend and coming to spend the weekend with her. At the minute the evening reached what she considered its peak of mellowness, she intended to speak to her father and mother about the festival and Bernadine's visit. She was exceedingly uncertain about their performances on both these occasions.

The rain suddenly began to fall harder. Cress' father, hearing it on the roof, watched with gratification[1] as the water streamed across the dark windowpanes. "Just what the oranges have been a-thirsting for," he said.

Mrs. Delahanty closed her book. "How's the schedule coming?" she asked her husband.

"OK, I guess," said Mr. Delahanty.

Cress looked up from the festival program with embarrassment. The schedule was one of the things she wanted to speak to her father about. She hoped he wouldn't mention it while Bernadine was visiting them. Every winter, as work on the ranch slackened, he drew up a schedule for the better ordering of his life. And every spring, as work picked up, he abandoned it as easily as if it had never been. Last winter, he had made a plan called "A Schedule of Exercises to Ensure Absolute Fitness" which included not only the schedule of exercises and the hours at which he proposed to practice them but a list of the weaknesses they were to counteract. He had even gone so far, last winter, as to put on a pair of peculiar short pants and run six times around the orchard without stopping, arms flailing, chest pumping — a very embarrassing sight, and one that Cress could not possibly have explained to Bernadine.

This winter, the subject of her father's schedule-making was not in itself so unsuitable. He had bought a new encyclopedia set and was mapping out a reading program that would enable him, by a wise use of his spare time, to cover the entire field of human knowledge in a year. The name of the schedule, written at the top of a sheet of Cress' yellow graph paper, was, in fact, "Human Knowledge in a Year." There was nothing about this plan that would call for embarrassing public action, like running around the orchard in shorts, but it was so incredibly naïve and dreamy that Cress hoped her father would not speak of it. Bernadine was far too sophisticated for schedules.

"Where are you now on your schedule, John?" Mrs. Delahanty asked.

Mr. Delahanty, who liked to talk about his plans almost as much as he liked to make them, put down his pen and picked up the sheet of paper on which he had been writing. "I've got all the subjects I want to read up about listed, and the times I'll have free *for* reading listed. Nothing left to do now but decide what's the best time for what. For instance, if you were me, Gertrude, would you spend the fifteen minutes before breakfast on art? Or on archeology, say?"

"You don't ever have fifteen minutes before breakfast," Mrs. Delahanty said.

Mr. Delahanty picked up his pen. "I thought you wanted to discuss this."

"Oh, I do!" said Mrs. Delahanty. "Well, if I had fifteen minutes before breakfast, *I'd* read about archeology."

"Why?" asked Mr. Delahanty.

"It's more orderly that way," Mrs. Delahanty said.

"Orderly?" asked Mr. Delahanty.

"A-r-c," Mrs. Delahanty spelled, "comes before a-r-t."

Mr. Delahanty made an impatient sound. "I'm not going at this alphabetically, Gertrude. Cut and dried. What I'm thinking about is what would make the most interesting morning reading. The most interesting and inspiring."

"Art is supposed to be more inspiring," Mrs. Delahanty told him. "If that's what you're after."

This seemed to decide Mr. Delahanty. "No, I think science should be the morning subject," he said, and wrote something at the top of a sheet — "Science," Cress supposed. "That's better," he said. "That leaves art for the evening, when I'll have time to read aloud to you."

"Don't change your schedule around for my sake, John," said Mrs. Delahanty, who hated being read to about anything.

"I'm not. All personal considerations aside, that's a more logical arrangement. Now the question is, which art?"

This seemed to Cress the moment for which she had been waiting. "Dancing is one of the earliest and most important of the arts," she said quickly.

"Oho!" said her father. "I thought you were in a coma."

"I've been rehearsing," said Cress.

"Rehearsing!" exclaimed Mr. Delahanty.

"In my mind," Cress said.

"So that's what was going on — 'Ladies' Whim,' 'Tsigan-otchka.' "

"Father," Cress interrupted, "I've told you and told you the t's silent. Why don't you take the program and practice the names? I'll help you." Cress got up and took the program across to her father.

"Practice them?" said Mr. Delahanty with surprise, reading through the dances listed. "What do I care how they're pronounced? 'Korbushka,' 'Kohanotchka,' " he said, mispronouncing wildly. "I'm not going to Russia."

"But you're going to the folk-dance festival," Cress reminded him.

"I don't *have* to go. If you don't want — "

"I do, Father. You know I want you to go. Only I don't want you to mispronounce the names."

"Look, Cress," Mr. Delahanty said. "I promise you I'll keep my mouth shut the whole time I'm there. No one will know you have a father who can't pronounce. Mute[2] I'll come and mute I'll go."

"I don't want you to be mute," Cress protested. "And even if I did, you couldn't very well be mute the whole time Bernadine's here. Bernadine's going to be a great star."

"A great dancer?" Mrs. Delahanty asked.

"She hasn't decided what kind of an artist yet," Cress said.

72

"The achievement of the impossible."

"Only to be great in something."

"Well, well," said Mr. Delahanty. "I'm beginning to look forward to meeting Bernadine."

"You already have," Cress told him. "Bernadine was one of the girls who rode with us to the basketball game."

Mr. Delahanty squinted his eyes, as if trying to peer backward to the Friday two weeks before when he had provided Cress and four of her friends with transportation to an out-of-town game. He shook his head. "Can't recall any Bernadine," he said.

"She was the one in the front seat with us," Cress reminded him.

"That girl!" exclaimed Mr. Delahanty, remembering. "But her name wasn't Bernadine, was it?"

"No," Cress told him. "That's what I wanted to explain to you, because tomorrow's Friday, too."

Mr. Delahanty left desk and schedule and walked over in front of the fireplace. From this position, he could get a direct view of his daughter.

"What's this you're saying, Cress?" he asked. "Her name isn't Bernadine because tomorrow's Friday? Is that what you said?"

"Yes, it is," Cress told him, seriously. "Only it's not just tomorrow. Her name isn't Bernadine on any Friday.''

Mr. Delahanty appealed to his wife. "Do you hear what I hear, Gertrude?''

"Mother,'' Cress protested, "this isn't anything funny. In fact, it's a complete tragedy.''

"Well, Cress dear,'' her mother said reasonably, "I haven't said a word. And your father's just trying to get things straight.''

"He's trying to be funny about a tragedy,'' Cress insisted obstinately.[3]

"Now, Cress,'' Mr. Delahanty urged, "you're jumping to conclusions. Though I admit I think it's queer to have a name on Fridays you don't have the rest of the week. And I don't see anything tragic about it.''

"That's what I'm trying to tell you, only you keep acting as if it's a joke.''

"What is Bernadine's name on Fridays, Cress?'' asked her mother.

"Nedra,'' said Cress solemnly.

Mr. Delahanty snapped his fingers. "Yes, sir,'' he said, "that's it! That's what they called her, all right.''

"Of course,'' said Cress. "Everyone does on Fridays, out of respect for her sorrow.''

"Just what *is* Bernadine's sorrow, Cress?'' her mother asked.

"Bernadine never did say — out and out, that is. Once in a while she tries to. But she just can't. It overwhelms her. But we all know what, generally speaking, must have happened.''

"What?'' asked Mr. Delahanty. "Generally speaking?''

Cress looked at her father suspiciously, but his face was all sympathetic concern.

"On some Friday in the past,'' she said, "Nedra had to say no to someone. Someone she loved.''

"How old is Berna — Nedra?'' Mrs. Delahanty asked.

"Sixteen,'' Cress said. "Almost.''

"Well, it couldn't have been too long ago then, could it?'' her mother suggested.

"Was this person,'' Mr. Delahanty ventured, "this person Nedra said no to, a male?''

"Of course,'' said Cress. "I told you it was a complete tragedy, didn't I? His name was Ned. That much we know.''

"Then the Nedra is in honor of — Ned?'' asked her mother.

"In honor and loving memory," Cress told her. "On the very next Friday, Ned died."

Mr. Delahanty said nothing. Mrs. Delahanty said, "Poor boy!"

"I think he was probably more than a boy," Cress said. "He owned two drugstores."

After the elder Delahantys had thought about this for a while, Mr. Delahanty asked, "This 'no' Bernadine — Nedra — said, was it to a proposal of marriage?"

"We don't ever ask about that," Cress told her father disapprovingly. "It doesn't seem like good taste to us."

"No, I don't suppose it is," Mr. Delahanty admitted.

"Anyway," Cress said, "that's Bernadine's tragedy and we all respect it and her wish to be called Nedra on Fridays. And tomorrow is a Friday, and it would be pretty awful to have her upset before the festival."

Mr. Delahanty stepped briskly back to his desk. "Don't you worry for a second, Cress," he said. "As far as I'm concerned, the girl's name is Nedra."

"Thank you, Father," Cress said. "I knew you'd understand. Now I'd better go to bed." At the door to the hallway, she turned and spoke once again. "If I were you, Father, I wouldn't say anything about your schedule to Bernadine."

"I hadn't planned on talking to her about it. But what's wrong with it?" Mr. Delahanty sounded a little testy.[4]

"Oh, nothing," Cress assured him. "I think it's dear and sweet of you to make schedules. Only it's so idealistic."

After Cress left the room, Mr. Delahanty said, "What's wrong with being idealistic?"

Cress thought that her friend, in her costume for "Fado Blanquita," the Spanish dance in which she performed the solo part, looked like the queen of grace and beauty. And she said so.

"This does rather suit my type," Bernadine admitted. She was leaning out from the opened casement window of Cress's room into the shimmering, rain-washed air. She tautened her costume's already tight bodice,[5] fluffed up its already bouffant[6] skirt, and extended her hands in one of the appealing gestures of the dance toward the trees of the orange orchard.

"Is your father a shy man?" she asked.

Mr. Delahanty, who had been working near the driveway to the

"She saw herself through other eyes than her own."

house when the two girls got off the school bus an hour before, had, instead of lingering to greet them, quickly disappeared behind a row of trees. Now, in rubber boots, carrying a light spade that he was using to test the depth to which the night before's rain had penetrated the soil, he came briefly into sight, waved his spade, and once again disappeared.

"No," said Cress, who thought her father rather bold, if anything. "He's just busy. After the rain, you know."

"Rain, sunshine. Sunshine, rain," Bernadine said understandingly. She moved her hands about in the placid[7] afternoon air as if scooping up samples. "Farming is an awfully elemental[8] life, I expect. My father" — Bernadine's father, J. M. Deevers, was vice-president of the Tenant First National Bank — "probably doesn't know one element from another. I expect your father's rather an elemental type, too, isn't he? Fundamentally, I mean?"

"I don't know, Nedra," Cress said humbly.

"He's black-haired," Bernadine said. "It's been my experience that black-haired men are very elemental." She brought her expressive hands slowly down to her curving red satin bodice. "You must have a good deal of confidence in your family to let them go tonight," she went on briskly.

"Let them!" Cress repeated, amazed at the word.

"Perhaps they're different from my family. Mine always keep me on pins and needles about what they're going to say and do next."

"Mine, too," Cress admitted, though loyalty to her father and mother would not permit her to say how greatly they worried her. She never went any place with them that she was not filled with a tremulous[9] concern lest they do or say something that would discredit them all. She stayed with them. She attempted to guide them. She harkened to every word said to them, so that she could prompt them with the right answers. But *let* them! "They always just take it for granted that where I go, they go," she said. "There's not much question of letting."

"Mine used to be that way," Bernadine confided. "But after what happened at the festival last year, I put my foot down. 'This year,' I told them, 'you're not going.' "

"What happened last year?" asked Cress, who had not been a dancer.

"After the program was over last year, Miss Ingols asked for parent participation in the dancing. And my father participated. He danced the 'Hopak,' and pretty soon he was lifting Miss Ingols off the floor at every other jump."

"Oh, Nedra," Cress said. "How terrible! What did Ingols do?"

"Nothing," said Bernadine. "That was the disgusting part. As a matter of fact, she seemed to enjoy it. But you can imagine how I suffered."

Cress nodded. She could. She was thinking how she would suffer if her father, in addition to mispronouncing all the dances, went out on the gymnasium floor and, before all her friends, misdanced them.

"Are your parents the participating type?" Bernadine asked.

Cress nodded with sad conviction. "Father is. And Mother is if encouraged."

"You'd better warn them right away," Bernadine said. "Your father just came in the back door. You could warn him now."

Cress walked slowly down the hallway toward the kitchen. Before the evening was over, her father, too, would probably be jouncing Miss Ingols around, and even calling Bernadine Bernadine — then all would be ruined completely, all she had looked forward to for so long. In the kitchen, she noted signs of the special supper her mother

77

was cooking because of Bernadine: the cole-slaw salad had shreds of green peppers and red apples mixed through it tonight to make it festive. The party sherbet glasses, with their long, icicle stems, awaited the lemon pudding. But her mother was out of the kitchen — on the back porch telling her father to hurry, because they would have to have dinner early if they were to get to the festival in time. "Festival!" Cress heard her father say. "I wish I'd never heard of that festival. How did Cress ever come to get mixed up in this dancing business, anyway?" he asked. "She's no dancer. Why, the poor kid can hardly get through a room without knocking something over. Let alone dance!"

"That's *why* she's mixed up with it," her mother explained. "To overcome her awkwardness. And she *is* better."

"But is she good enough?" asked her father. "I'd hate to think of her making a spectacle of herself — to say nothing of having to sit and watch it."

"Now, John," Cress heard her mother say soothingly. "You're always too concerned about Cress. Will she do this right? Will she do that right? Stop worrying. Cress'll probably be fine."

"Maybe fall on her ear, too," her father said morosely.[10] "They oughtn't to put so much responsibility on kids. Performing in public. Doesn't it worry you any?"

"Certainly it worries me. But all parents worry. And remember, we'll have the star of the performance with us. You can concentrate on Nedra if watching Cress is too much for you."

"That Nedra! The only dance I can imagine that girl doing is one in which she would carry somebody's head on a platter."

Cress had started back down the hall before her father had finished this sentence, but she had not gone so far as to miss its final word. She stopped in the bathroom to have a drink of water and to see how she looked in the mirror over the washbasin. She looked different. For the first time in her life, she saw herself through other eyes than her own. Through her parents' eyes. Did parents worry about the figures their *children* cut? Were they embarrassed for *them*, and did they wonder if they were behaving suitably, stylishly, well? Cress felt a vacant, hollow space beneath her heart, which another glass of water did nothing to fill. Why *I'm* all right, Cress thought. *I* know how to behave. I'll get by. *They're* the ones . . . but she looked at her face again and it was wavering, doubtful — not the triumphant face she had imagined, smiling in sureness as she danced the come-and-go figures of "Road to the Isles."

She went back to her room full of thought. Bernadine was changing her costume, and her muffled voice came from under all her skirts. "Did you tell them?" this muffled voice asked.

"No," said Cress, "I didn't."

"Why not? Won't you be worried?"

"They're the ones who are worrying. About me."

"About you?"

"Father thinks I may fall on my ear."

Bernadine, clear of her skirts, nodded in smiling agreement. "It's a possibility that sometimes occurs to *me*, Cress dear."

Cress gazed at her friend speculatively.[11] "They're worried about you, too," she said.

"Me?" asked Bernadine, her smile fading.

"Father said the only dance he could imagine you doing was one with a head on a platter."

"Salome!" Bernadine exclaimed with pleasure. "Your father's imaginative, isn't he? Sympathetically imaginative?"

"I guess so," Cress said, and in her confusion told everything. "He keeps schedules."

"Schedules?"

"For the better ordering of his life."

Bernadine laughed again. "How precious!" she said.

Then, as if remembering after too long a lapse the day and her bereavement, she said, "Neddy was like that, too."

"Neddy," repeated Cress, pain for the present making Bernadine's past seem not only past but silly. "Oh, shut up about Neddy, *Bernadine!*"

Bernadine gave a little gasp. "Have you forgotten it's Friday?"

"I don't care what day it is," Cress said. She walked over to her bed, picked up the pillow and lay down. Then she put the pillow over her face.

---

[1] **gratification:** the state of being gratified; satisfaction
[2] **mute:** silent
[3] **obstinately:** stubbornly
[4] **testy:** annoyed; irritated
[5] **bodice:** waist of a woman's dress
[6] **bouffant:** puffed out
[7] **placid:** calm; peaceful
[8] **elemental:** reduced to essentials; basic
[9] **tremulous:** trembling

[10] **morosely:** in a gloomy manner
[11] **speculatively:** thoughtfully; reflectively

A CLOSER LOOK

1. Why is this dance concert important to Cress? Why is she eager to get along with Bernadine?

2. Do you think Mr. Delahanty is unusual or eccentric? Compare the Delahanty family to Bernadine's family. Why does Cress change her mind about her parents?

3. Who would you rather have as a friend, Bernadine or Cress? Why?

John Steinbeck

BREAKFAST

● Imagine yourselves back in the Great Depression of the early 1930s. Droughts have turned the Great Plains into a Dust Bowl. Farmers and their families are traveling on foot or in old battered trucks piled high with all their possessions, drifting wherever temporary day labor is being hired. Under these circumstances, the offering of breakfast to a stranger takes on special meaning.

THIS THING FILLS ME WITH PLEASURE. I DON'T know why, I can see it in the smallest detail. I find myself recalling it again and again, each time bringing more detail out of a sunken memory; remembering brings the curious warm pleasure.

It was very early in the morning. The eastern mountains were black-blue, but behind them the light stood up faintly colored at the mountain rims with a washed red, growing colder, grayer and darker as it went up and overhead until, at a place near the west, it merged with pure night.

And it was cold, not painfully so, but cold enough so that I rubbed my hands and shoved them deep into my pockets, and I hunched my shoulders up and scuffled my feet on the ground. Down in the valley where I was, the earth was that lavender gray of dawn. I walked along a country road and ahead of me I saw a tent that was only a little lighter gray than the ground. Beside the tent, there was a flash of orange fire seeping out of the cracks of an old rusty iron stove. Gray smoke spurted up out of the stubby stovepipe, spurted up a

"There was some element of great beauty there."

long way before it spread out and dissipated.[1]

I saw a young woman beside the stove, really a girl. She was dressed in a faded cotton skirt and waist. As I came close, I saw that she carried a baby in a crooked arm and the baby was nursing, its head under her waist out of the cold. The mother moved about, poking the fire, shifting the rusty lids of the stove to make a greater draft, opening the oven door; and all the time the baby was nursing, but that didn't interfere with the mother's work, nor with the light, quick gracefulness of her movements. There was something very precise and practiced in her movements. The orange fire flicked out of the cracks in the stove and threw dancing reflections on the tent.

I was close now and I could smell frying bacon and baking bread, the warmest, pleasantest odors I know. From the east the light grew swiftly. I came near to the stove and stretched my hands out to it and shivered all over when the warmth struck me. Then the tent flap jerked up and a young man came out and an older man followed him. They were dressed in new blue dungarees and in new dungaree coats with the brass buttons shining. They were sharp-faced men, and they looked much alike.

The younger had a dark stubble beard and the older had a gray stubble beard. Their heads and faces were wet, their hair dripped with water, and water stood out on their stiff beards and their cheeks shone with water. Together they stood looking quietly at the lightening east; they yawned together and looked at the light on the hill rims. They turned and saw me.

"Morning," said the older man. His face was neither friendly nor unfriendly.

"Morning, sir," I said.

The water was slowly drying on their faces. They came to the stove and warmed their hands at it.

The girl kept to her work, her face averted[2] and her eyes on what she was doing. Her hair was tied back out of her eyes with a string and it hung down her back and swayed as she worked. She set tin cups on a big packing box, set tin plates and knives and forks out, too. Then she scooped fried bacon out of the deep grease and laid it on a big tin platter, and the bacon cricked and rustled as it grew crisp. She opened the rusty oven door and took out a square pan full of high big biscuits.

When the smell of that hot bread came out, both of the men inhaled deeply.

The elder man turned to me, "Had your breakfast?"

"No."

"Well, sit down with us, then."

That was the signal. We went to the packing case and squatted on the ground about it. The young man asked, "Picking cotton?"

"No."

"We had twelve days' work so far," the young man said.

The girl spoke from the stove. "They even got new clothes."

The two men looked down at their new dungarees and they both smiled a little.

The girl set out the platter of bacon, the brown high biscuits, a bowl of bacon gravy and a pot of coffee, and then she squatted down by the box, too. The baby was still nursing, its head up under her waist out of the cold. I could hear the sucking noises it made.

We filled our plates, poured bacon gravy over our biscuits and sugared our coffee. The older man filled his mouth full, and he chewed and chewed and swallowed. Then . . . he filled his mouth again.

The young man said, "We been eating good for twelve days."

We all ate quickly, frantically, and refilled our plates and ate quickly again until we were full and warm. The hot bitter coffee scalded our throats. We threw the last little bit with the grounds in it on the earth and refilled our cups.

There was color in the light now, a reddish gleam that made the air seem colder. The two men faced the east and their faces were lighted by the dawn, and I looked up for a moment and saw the image of the mountain and the light coming over it reflected in the older man's eyes.

Then the two men threw the grounds from their cups on the earth and they stood up together. "Got to get going," the older man said.

The younger turned to me." 'Fyou want to pick cotton, we could maybe get you on."

"No. I got to go along. Thanks for breakfast."

The older man waved his hand in a negative. "O.K. Glad to have you." They walked away together. The air was blazing with light at the eastern skyline. And I walked away down the country road.

That's all. I know, of course, some of the reasons why it was pleasant. But there was some element of great beauty there that makes the rush of warmth when I think of it.

[1] **dissipated:** separated into parts; thinned out and vanished
[2] **averted:** turned aside

A CLOSER LOOK

1. What happens in the story that fills the narrator with pleasure? Do you agree that what takes place has an element of great beauty in it? Why or why not?

2. Do you think that these people would have acted differently if they were not poor? If so, in what ways?

3. If a hungry stranger came by just as you were getting ready to eat breakfast, would you ask him to share your meal? Why or why not?

• Mothers often do things for their children that no one else would do, and expect no reward for it. Why do some women sacrifice themselves like this? The poem doesn't exactly explain why, but its tone of tenderness and joy is perhaps an answer in itself.

Myra Sklarew

POEM OF THE MOTHER

The heart goes out ahead
scouting for him
while I stay at home
keeping the fire,
holding the house down
around myself
like a skirt from the high wind.

The boy does not know
how my eye strains to make out
his small animal shape
swimming hard across the future
nor that I have strengthened myself
like the wood side of this house
for his benefit.

"I love that girl. What have I ever given her?"

Paddy Chayefsky

THE BIG DEAL

• In the 1950s, Paddy Chayefsky was one of the first important writers to work in television. He showed that the small home screen was ideally suited to strong dramas that examined the everyday lives of ordinary people, struggling with moral problems. "The Big Deal" is a realistic story of a man whose life has reached a crisis. But it's not only about him — it's about all the people around him who care what happens to him.

CHARACTERS

JOE MANX	SECOND WORKMAN
DAUGHTER (MARILYN)	THIRD WORKMAN
GEORGE	SAM HARVARD
WIFE (DORIS)	COMPLAINER
FRANK DAUGHERTY	WELL-DRESSED MAN
FIRST WORKMAN	HARRY GERBER

ACT I

FADE IN:

Restaurant — not too posh, but the tables have linen tablecloths. The general effect is of a crowded café. We narrow our attention to a little man of fifty-odd years, seated at a table, studying a cup of coffee in front of him. He has on a blue pencil-stripe suit, single-breasted, which somehow gives the feeling of the 1930s. His tie is tied into a narrow, elegant knot; but it is slightly askew. His shirt collar turns up at the edges. This is JOE MANX. *He looks up, and his face perks up a bit as he recognizes someone approaching his*

*table. A moment later a pretty girl of twenty-six comes to his table.
She bends over him and gives him a quick kiss.*

Marilyn: Hello, Pa.

Joe: Sit down, Marilyn, sit down. You want something to eat?
Eggs, a sandwich, anything like that?

Marilyn *(sitting)*: No, Pa, I'm meeting George for lunch in about
fifteen minutes.

Joe: Sure. Give him my regards when you see him. I won't hold
you. I happen to need about ten, fifteen dollars if you happen to
have it on you.

Marilyn *(promptly opening her purse)*: Sure, Pa.

Joe: I ran across a very interesting proposition today, and I'd like to
take the man out for a couple of drinks. I have an appointment
with him at four o'clock.

Marilyn *(extracting some bills from her purse)*: Are you sure fifteen
bucks will be enough?

Joe: Oh, plenty, plenty. I'm just going to take him for a couple of
drinks. *(He takes the bills.)* I might be able to pay you this back
on Thursday, because I'm playing a little pinochle over at Harry
Gerber's tomorrow night, and I usually come out a couple of
bucks ahead. Listen, Marilyn, don't let me hold you. I know
you're anxious to get to see George.

Marilyn: All right, Pa. I'll see you later.

Joe: Just let me say that this is a very interesting proposition that I
ran across today. I don't want to sound premature, but I have a
feeling that this might be the deal I've been looking for. I won't
bore you with the details. I only want to say this proposition
involves Louie Miles, if the name is at all familiar to you. He
happens to be one of the biggest contractors in the business.
Eighteen years ago, he was a lousy little plasterer. I gave him his
first work. Well, I was down at the Municipal Building today. It
happened that I . . . Well, look, I don't want to hold you. I can
see you're anxious to see your boyfriend. Go ahead, go ahead.
Give him my regards. Don't tell your mother you gave me some
money.

Marilyn *(who has been smiling fondly at her father throughout his
speech)*: Okay, Pa, I'll see you.

Joe: I'll see you. I'll see you. Have a good lunch. *(MARILYN
exits. JOE sits a moment, fingering the two bills his daughter has*

just given him. Then he suddenly lifts a hand and calls out sharply.) Waiter! Check!

DISSOLVE TO:

A booth in another restaurant. We see MARILYN *and a young resident doctor named* GEORGE. *He is wearing the conventional white-jacketed uniform. They have their pie and coffee in front of them — also the dishes of the meal they have just eaten, which have not been taken away yet.* MARILYN *is eating her pie, but* GEORGE *is just fiddling with his fork. They are both obviously caught in a deep discussion.*

Marilyn: I know these aren't ideal times to get married in. But who gets married in ideal times? You know what I mean?

George: I know, I know.

Marilyn: Everybody has problems when they get married. They got parents to support, and they don't have enough money. These are just things everybody has to face when they get married.

George: Yeah. Well, let's get married and get it over with.

Marilyn: You make it sound awful.

George: Look, Marilyn, marriage is serious business. I've got two more years of residency. You're going to have to support me for two years.

Marilyn: I'm making a good salary, George.

George: You're already supporting your mother and father.

Marilyn: I've got five thousand dollars that my Aunt Eva left me.

George: Look, Marilyn. You want to get married, it's all right with me. *(MARILYN frowns down at her plate.)* I mean it. We'll go to City Hall and get married. What do we need? Blood tests. All right, I'll take you to the blood lab right now. Do we have to wait three days? All right, we'll get married on Friday. *(They both look down at their plates.)* My mother is against this marriage. You know that, don't you? Even my old man, who likes you a lot, says I can't afford to take on a wife.

Marilyn: Take on a wife! What am I, a bundle you're to carry on your back?

George: I didn't mean it that way.

Marilyn: What do you think marriage is? Death in a gas chamber? Marriage is making somebody happy. You get better from marriage, not worse. Maybe you might find the next two years a little

"You just forget how much you love the girl."

easier if you had somebody near you who wants you to be happy. I don't care if I have to support half of Toledo, Ohio! It's no sacrifice to me if it makes you happy! And I expect the same from you!

(She hides her eyes in her hand and tries to master herself. GEORGE sits in the sudden vacuum left by MARILYN's outburst, looking down at his hands folded in his lap.)

George *(rises — crosses around table — sits beside her)*: Marilyn, honestly, I don't know why I'm making such a crisis out of this. I'm a little scared, that's all. You just forget how much you love the girl. I would like to officially set our wedding for this coming Friday, if you'll have me, and I promise to make you happy. So what do you say?

Marilyn: I finally collared you, eh?

George *(beaming)*: Yeah.

DISSOLVE TO:

The front hallway of a four-and-a-half-room apartment. We are

looking at the front door, which now opens and admits JOE MANX.
*He closes the door behind him, takes off his hat, puts it on the mail
table. Then, carrying himself with a sort of bantam[1] erectness, he
passes into the living room.*

*The living room is furnished with what had been good, solid,
expensive middle-class furniture two decades ago. The dominating
piece in the living room is a large, dark, mahogany table. At the
head of the table is a massive chair with thick armrests. It is to this
chair that* JOE *marches. He takes off his jacket, drapes it around the
back of the chair, rolls up his shirt-sleeves two turns, loosens his tie,
unbuttons his collar, and then sits down in the chair, placing his
arms on the armrests. For a moment he just sits there, enjoying a
small feeling of majesty. Then he lifts his head and calls out.*

Joe: I'm home!

(His wife DORIS *appears in the kitchen doorway. She is a strong
woman of about fifty. On her face there is the smile of someone
who is about to share a secret. Her secret becomes immediately
apparent when* MARILYN *appears behind her in the kitchen
doorway.)*

Doris: Joe, I got a pleasant shock to tell you. So get a good hold on
your chair. I don't want you to fall off and hit your head on the
floor.
Joe: I ran across a very big deal today.
Marilyn *(coming in)*: Hello, Pa.
Joe: I was down at the Municipal Building, and I walked over to the
water fountain.
Doris: Joe, listen . . .
Joe: Louis Miles comes over to me. Doris, you remember Louis
Miles? He was a plasterer.
Doris: Joe, listen.
Joe: It seems he's a big construction man now. So we got to talking.
He's bought fifteen acres of land near Willaston. He wanted to put
up sixty houses on the land. He started to dig and boom! He ran
into water. I told him I'd have known better than to let him do it.
Anyway, now he wants to sell the land. We made a date for four
o'clock at the Statler Hotel. *(to* MARILYN*)* Sweetheart, could
you get me a glass of water?

Marilyn: Sure. *(She goes into the kitchen.)*

Joe: Well, I began a little quick thinking. If I had one hundred and fifty acres of that land, I could put up a thousand houses. With a thousand houses, it's worth the expense of draining the water.

Doris: Joe, Marilyn also ran across a very big deal today.

Joe: I went to the Statler Hotel. I said, "Louie, why don't we buy up another hundred and fifty acres? We could put up a thousand houses instead of just sixty!" He acted like I was crazy.

Doris: He was right, too.

Joe: When I built all those houses before, people used to laugh, too. But I was a big success, wasn't I?

Doris: That was in 1934. Anyway, what happened with Louie Miles?

Joe: He wants to sell that fifteen acres. It will cost me four thousand dollars.

Doris: Did you see Harry Gerber?

Joe: Doris, I don't want to hear about Harry Gerber. And don't make fun of me.

Doris: I don't make fun of you.

Joe: You think I'm a big talker without a nickel to his name. All right, I'm broke. But I was once the biggest builder in this city. Before I'm dead, I'll make a million dollars and leave it to you.

(MARILYN enters with water.)

Marilyn: Pa, I'm getting married Friday.

Joe *(shocked)*: When did this happen?

Marilyn: At lunch, after I saw you.

Doris: I told you we had a shock for you.

Joe: For heaven's sake! Which one is this? The doctor? George? *(MARILYN nods.)* Well, this calls for some kind of celebration. Call him up on the phone. Tell him to come over tonight.

Marilyn: He's on duty.

Joe: I'm taking us out for a real celebration.

Marilyn: He's coming over tomorrow night, Pa.

Joe *(staring at DORIS)*: What are you sitting there in a house dress for? Your daughter's getting married.

Doris: I just found out myself fifteen minutes ago.

Joe: What's the fanciest restaurant in town?

Doris: I got chicken in the stove now.

Joe: We'll eat it cold tomorrow. Doris, put on a dress with feathers on it. Joe Manx's daughter gets married, this town is going to hear about it.

Marilyn *(laughing)*: All right, Ma. I feel like celebrating, too.

(DORIS goes out. MARILYN goes into the kitchen to turn off the stove. JOE follows her.)

Joe: George is a nice young fellow. He'll soon be making thirty thousand bucks a year. Several years ago, I would have given you two kids a wedding the whole town would talk about for weeks. *(pause)* Marilyn, I'll need a couple of bucks to cover the evening. It might come to as much as twenty-five dollars.

Marilyn: Sure, Pa. *(She gets purse in dining room, gives JOE money. He closes his eyes to keep from crying.)*

DISSOLVE TO:

JOE *and* DORIS' *bedroom, late that night. They are getting ready for bed.*

Doris: She's going to have to support her husband for a couple of years. She can't pay the rent on this house anymore. Maybe we'll have to move. We're not taking another penny from that girl. Harry Gerber says he has a job for you with the city.

Joe: If you want to know, I went to see Harry Gerber last week. Do you think I don't want a decent job? You think I like being supported by my daughter?

Doris: So what happened with Harry Gerber?

Joe: It was a lousy job he had for me. A building inspector. Fifteen thousand dollars a year. I'm not a fifteen-thousand-dollar-a-year-man! Doris, I was a big operator at one time!

Doris: That was fifteen years ago, Joe.

Joe: All right, I went broke. But I still got it in my head. I can't think in terms of fifteen thousand dollars a year.

Doris: Joe, how many businesses have you tried? You tried the trucking business. You tried others, too.

Joe: I was out of my field. I'm a builder.

Doris: I won't let you take any more money off that girl.

Joe: You want me to take this job as a lousy building inspector? I won't do it.

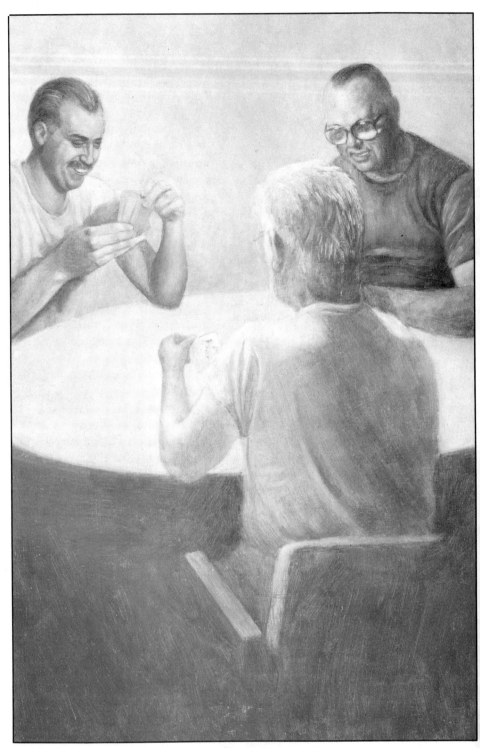

"I want to buy some land."

Doris: All right, Joe.

Joe: Don't worry about me, Doris. We're not going to take another penny of that girl. I love that girl. What have I ever given her? I couldn't even afford to send her to a decent college. I haven't even got a life-insurance policy so that she could benefit from my death.

Doris: Joe, don't be so dramatic. We had money once. We don't have it anymore. You've had a long time to get used to that fact.

Joe (*pounding the bed table*): I'm going to leave that girl a million dollars in my will!

Doris: Fifteen thousand dollars a year would suit us fine. Why do we need more?

Joe: There's a million-dollar deal in that Willaston land. Right now, all I need is four thousand dollars. I'll get it from Frank Daugherty tomorrow. He's a good friend who owes me favors. And I'll get some money from Sam Harvard, too. I could make two hundred thousand dollars! This is a very interesting deal!

ACT II

FADE IN:

Construction work is going on in a city. A high wooden fence has been erected around the large corner area of the construction. Towering above the fence are the skeletal girders of the proposed building. We hear the noise and sounds of construction. The camera pans slowly across this view and up and onto a huge wooden sign on which is written:

A NEW 12-STORY OFFICE BUILDING
WILL BE ERECTED ON THIS SITE —
TO BE COMPLETED SEPTEMBER 1953.
FRANK DAUGHERTY AND SONS,
GENERAL CONTRACTORS

Close-up shot of the name of Daugherty.

CUT TO:

Interior, construction shack, crudely furnished. A wooden table is piled with papers, blueprints, and a portable typewriter. Coveralls hang from wall nails. On the wall is a drawing of the proposed office building with Daugherty's name in bold printed letters at the bottom.

Two men are in the shop, both in their forties. Both wear baggy suits and hats, despite the fact that it is a July day. They are leaning over a large blueprint spread out on the table, muttering to each other. Suddenly one bursts out:

First Man: So what are we gonna do with all those guys sittin' out there?
Second Man: Nothin'. The reinforcement rods aren't here yet.

(The two men return to the blueprint. There is a knock at the door.)

Second Man *(without looking up, barks out)*: Come in! *(The door opens and JOE MANX comes in, dressed as he was in Act I. He closes the door behind him.)*
Second Man *(turns to JOE)*: Wadda you want, mister?
Joe: I'm waiting for Frank Daugherty.
Second Man: Wadda you wanna see him about?
Joe: I have a personal matter I want to see him about.
Second Man: You can't wait in here. Wait outside.
First Man: Oh, he's gonna blow the roof off about those rods, boy. I told him yesterday, they ain't gonna be here, and he said . . . *(The door opens and a tall, angular Irishman of about fifty comes in.)* Listen, Frank, the rods didn't come in yet. I got a whole crew outside waiting to get started. You told me yesterday, get them ready for the morning.
Daugherty: Where's Andy?
Second Man: I don't know. He ain't here yet, either.
Daugherty *(to the FIRST MAN)*: Get Andy on the phone for me. *(to JOE)* Hello, Manx. Wadda you want?
Joe: I'd like to have a couple of minutes alone with you.
Daugherty: I ain't got time now, Manx. *(JOE looks at DAUGHERTY, then at the scowling faces of the other two men.)*
Joe: I need four thousand dollars, Daugherty. I got a very big deal. I can get a piece of land.
Daugherty: What land?
Joe: Fifteen acres in the Willaston area.
Daugherty: Not interested.

Joe: Daugherty, I know it's wet land. But think in terms of a thousand houses.

Daugherty: The land won't hold houses. Louie Miles was here yesterday, trying to sell me that land. I tell you what I told Louie. I'm not interested. *(He goes to the door.)* Are we going to have to pay the workmen while we're waiting for the rods?

Second Man: Yeah.

Daugherty: Call the union. Manx, that land won't hold any kind of foundation. I told Louie Miles to try and sell it to the city. That land might hold some tennis courts. That's about all it's good for.

Joe: I think you're making a mistake, Daugherty.

Daugherty: It won't be the first time.

DISSOLVE TO:
Restaurant. SAM HARVARD *sits at a table with* JOE.

Harvard: Joe, why do you always hit me for these big deals of yours?

Joe: I came to you because —

Harvard: You came to me five years ago with some crazy deal about going into the trucking line. I gave you two thousand dollars then. I knew it was money out the window. And wasn't there something once about a tool-and-die plant you wanted to invest in? That cost me a thousand, I think. Joe, why don't you hit someone else for a change?

Joe: Sam, I'm going to tell you the truth. I went to Daugherty and some others. They're all getting old. They only want surefire deals. I didn't want to come to you, Sam. I know I owe you money.

Harvard: I don't need the money. But Joe, don't ask me for another four thousand dollars. Not for such a crazy deal as houses in Willaston.

Joe: I just want to remind you, I built houses before. I'm not a baby in this game. Go walk in the Chestnut Street area. Before I poured a footing there, the whole area was snakes and frogs. The grass was so high you could get lost·

(HARVARD breaks off a piece of Danish, looks up from under his heavy brows.)

Harvard: Joe, the answer is no. *(He sips his coffee and chews slowly and methodically. We fade out.)*

DISSOLVE TO:
JOE's *apartment. The dining room.* DORIS *and* MARILYN *are talking.*

Doris *(setting table)*: He's not coming home for dinner. So let's just have the cold chicken from yesterday and some vegetables I've got boiling. Is that all right with you?

Marilyn: That's fine with me. *(She goes to the kitchen and comes back with chicken.)*

Doris *(sitting at end of table)*: I'm worried about your father. He's beginning to talk like a fool. Five years ago, we listened to his big deals. We said maybe some of his friends would help him out. But now, he's beginning to sound like a comic character.

Marilyn: He's all right, Ma.

Doris: Do you think so? I don't think so. I think something terrible is going to happen to him. He doesn't talk like a completely sensible person anymore. I look at him sometimes; it seems to me he's in another world, dreaming.

(MARILYN sits across from her mother, studies the dish before her.)

Marilyn: He was a big shot once. It's hard for a man his age to change to new situations.

Doris: It's not a new situation. It's fifteen years old. He's got to understand that it's not important to be the governor's best friend. He was always the big spender. Even on our dates, he always took me to the most expensive places. I never knew where he got his money for such expensive dates. He never had a job in his life. He was always in this business or that business. He was the first one in our whole crowd to have a car. He was a generous man, your father. He had an open hand to everybody. We used to give big parties and fill the house with people. We don't give big parties anymore. He'll have to change. He's got to go out and earn a living, Marilyn.

Marilyn: Ma, why talk foolish? Where's he going to get a job?

Doris: Harry Gerber offered him a job.

"He sounds so depressed, Harry, make him take the job."

Marilyn: When was this?

Doris: A couple of weeks ago. It's a small job, a building inspector. It would be fine for us. He doesn't want to take it.

Marilyn: Ma, don't push him. He likes big things. It would kill him to be a little man. You're probably nagging him to take this job. You're thinking what a burden you and Pop are on me, especially now I'm getting married. It's no burden. I don't resent it.

Doris: Marilyn, you're not going to support Joe and me anymore.

Marilyn: Ma, I talked this out with George long ago. I'm going to take a couple of thousand out of Aunt Eva's money. We're going to put it down on a little house. You and Pop are going to live with us. George says it's perfectly okay with him. *(The doorbell rings.)* How much you want to bet that's George? *(She plucks a piece of chicken loose, rises, and goes to the door munching away. DORIS suddenly starts from her seat.)*

Doris: Oh, for goodness sakes, I forgot the vegetables. The water's probably all boiled out already. *(She hurries into the kitchen.)*

(MARILYN opens the door of the apartment. It is, indeed, GEORGE standing there.)

101

Marilyn: I knew it was you.

George: I haven't seen you in an hour. I missed you. Well, what are you going to do?

Marilyn: Come on in. You want some cold chicken? *(GEORGE comes in.* MARILYN *closes the door behind him.)*

George: Tell you the truth, I figured we might go to a restaurant tonight, have a celebration.

Marilyn: Come on in, sit down for a minute. *(She leads him back to the dining table, where they take seats.* MARILYN *calls to her mother in the kitchen.)* It's him again, Ma.

George *(calling)*: Hello, Mrs. Manx.

Doris *(off in kitchen)*: Hello, George. Give him some chicken, Marilyn.

Marilyn *(calling to* DORIS*)*: We're going to go out and eat, Ma, if you'll excuse us.

Doris *(in kitchen)*: Sure. Go ahead, go ahead. *(She appears in the kitchen doorway, holding a saucepan.)* I burned the vegetables anyway. Go on out. Have a good time. *(She disappears back into the kitchen.* MARILYN *and* GEORGE *sit for a minute.)*

Marilyn: My father was offered a job.

George: Yeah? Is he going to take it?

Marilyn: I don't think so, George. But it would be nice. I could even quit my job after a year. *(pause)* Well, what do you say? Is this dress okay for me to wear?

George: Sure. *(They start to leave.* GEORGE *calls into kitchen.)* Good-bye, Mrs. Manx.

Doris *(coming out)*: Good-bye, George. Good-bye, Marilyn. Have a nice time. *(They leave.* DORIS *picks up telephone and dials.)* Is this Harry Gerber? Harry, this is Doris Manx. Listen, Joe says he's coming over to your house for cards tonight. I'm worried about him, Harry. He sounds so depressed. Harry, make him take the job.

DISSOLVE TO:

HARRY GERBER's *living room. Four men sit around the table. On* JOE's *right sits the* COMPLAINER. *Directly across the table from* JOE *sits the* WELL-DRESSED MAN, *so named for reasons that will soon be obvious. On* JOE's *left sits* HARRY GERBER, *a heavyset, sympathetic man of fifty. The living room is comfortably furnished.* JOE *has apparently just won the last hand.*

Complainer: Gerber, why did you play the king? You knew he was sitting with an ace!

Well-Dressed Man: All right, how much did this hand cost me?

Gerber: Half a dollar. *(They put several half-dollars in a pile by* JOE.*)*

Complainer: How much do I owe you, Joe?

Joe: Half a dollar. *(He deals out the cards to each player.)*

Complainer *(pushing his two quarters over to* JOE*)*: I haven't won a hand all night, you know that? I get nothing but nines and jacks. Right now, all I want out of life is to see one flush.

Joe: Listen, I need four thousand dollars. Can you give it to me, you fellows?

Complainer: What?

Joe: What do you say? We've been playing pinochle together twenty years almost. Will you lend me four thousand dollars?

Complainer *(laughing)*: Lend it! Another couple of hands and you'll win it from me!

Well-Dressed Man: What do you need the money for, Joe? Are you in trouble?

Joe: I need it for a business deal. I want to buy some land.

Well-Dressed Man: Oh, land. Land I don't know anything about. If you were sick or in some kind of trouble, if you needed an operation or if you wanted to pay off a mortgage, something like that, I might be able to dig up a couple thousand for you. But land I'm not interested in. *(He studies his cards.)* Let's see. What's the bid to me?

Complainer: Gerber said three hundred. What do you say?

Well-Dressed Man: Three hundred is good with me.

Complainer: It's good with me, too. You want it, Harry, or not?

Gerber: Joe, what's this deal you want four thousand for?

Joe *(slams the table with his hand)*: Come on, Harry! Let's play cards! It's three hundred up to you! Do you want it or not?

Gerber *(without looking at his hand)*: I don't want it.

Joe: All right, throw in the hand. Here, deal. *(He pushes the discards, as they are thrown down, toward* GERBER.*)* Look, are we going to play cards, or are we going to talk! If we're going to play, let's play! If we're going to talk, let's talk! *(He suddenly stands, growing more frenzied.)* My friends! My friends! My good friends! Four lousy thousand bucks! You can't lend me four

"Any time you need me, you know you can come to me."

thousand lousy bucks! What am I, some kind of a bum or something? I built plenty of houses in my time! Good double-brick houses, three coats of plaster! *(He seizes the few bills and silver in front of him and scatters the money on the table.)* Here! A couple more bucks for you! *(He turns and walks out.* GERBER *rises quickly from his seat.)*

Gerber *(calling)*: Joe! *(He moves quickly after his friend.)*

DISSOLVE TO:

GERBER's *living room, later.* HARRY GERBER *and* JOE *are alone, drinking coffee.*

Joe: I went to them all, Harry. Daugherty brushed me off him like I was mud on his pants. What does this mean? Harry, will you tell me the truth?

Gerber: All right, I'll tell you the truth. You haven't got a name in this trade anymore. You're kidding yourself if you think you have. You can go on like this the rest of your life. Or you can face a couple of facts. I got a job for you. I tried to get you a desk job, but the flat truth is they wouldn't have you. I'm leveling with you,

Joe. Take it or leave it. It's fifteen thousand dollars a year. It'll pay your rent, and it'll give you a little self-respect. Joe, I'm your friend. Any time you need me, you know you can come to me. If I had four thousand dollars, I'd give it to you. But I would give it to you out of charity. I'd never expect to see any of it again.

Joe: Well, that's straight talk. I respect you for it. But I don't want your job.

Gerber: Are you ashamed to work for me?

Joe: Harry, you talk about facing facts. All right, let's face some facts. I failed as a man! I failed as a father! What did I ever give those two women? My wife wears the same cloth coat for four years, do you know that?

Gerber: You haven't failed anybody, Joe!

Joe: From the age of ten I never bought my daughter even a birthday present! She's getting married Friday. What will my wedding gift be? A house for the newlyweds? A ten-thousand-dollar bond? Do you know how it haunts me that I can't buy that girl something? What contempt she must have for me!

Gerber: Joe, you're talking like a fool. You're a wonderful father. Your girl is crazy about you. Stop torturing yourself.

Joe: Look, Harry, don't worry about me. I'm having a little rough time right now, but I'll come out of it. I'm fifty-two years old. Maybe I can't run around the block anymore, but I'm still operating where it counts.

Gerber: Joe, sit down a minute.

Joe: Apparently nobody has any faith in me, not even my best friend. Well, Harry, I'll dig up four thousand dollars somewheres, one way or another, and I'll buy fifteen lousy acres of swamp. . . . *(His voice is beginning to rise.)* And I'll show you what Joe Manx can do with it! I'll put the Empire State Building on that swamp! I'm a man of respect! Bricklayers like Frank Daugherty will come on their knees to kiss my hand! *(He suddenly smiles, but there is something almost wild about him.)* And, Harry, when I die, I'll leave fifteen thousand dollars a year for you in my will. *(He nods his head once or twice — then turns and stamps out of the room.)*

FADE OUT

ACT III

FADE IN:
The bedroom of JOE *and* DORIS MANX, *later that night. The room is dark. We fade in on* DORIS, *lying on her back on her bed, asleep. Suddenly her eyes open. Then her head slowly turns in the direction of her husband's bed. The camera slowly pans over to* JOE's *bed. It is empty. The blankets have been pushed aside, and the sheets are mussed — indicating that* JOE *has recently been sleeping there.*

DORIS *slowly sits up in bed, worried. She moves quickly around the beds to the door of the bedroom, opens it, passes into the dark hallway. She goes through the kitchen, opens that door, and steps into the living room.* JOE MANX *is seated in his large master chair, his arms resting on the armrests. He wears his trousers and bedroom slippers, but he has no shirt on. His hair is uncombed, and there is a distraught quality about him.*

Doris: I know, Joe, I know . . .

Joe: They're squeezing me here! You understand! They're squeezing me!

Doris: I understand, Joe.

Joe: Look at me, for goodness sake. They all make a living but me. What's the matter with me?

Doris: There's nothing the matter with you, Joe. *(He crosses to sofa, sits, slack and empty.)*

Joe: I would just like to close my eyes and wake up with another name, because I'm sick in my heart of being Joe Manx.

Doris: Joe, we don't want a million dollars from you. We love you, Joe, we love you if you build houses or if you don't build houses. We just want to have you around the house. We like to eat dinner with you. We like to see your face.

(JOE rises heavily from his seat and moves a few paces away. As he moves from DORIS, *he lets his hand rest lightly against her face in silent appreciation of her sympathy.)*

Joe *(muttering)*: I don't know, maybe there's something in this Las Vegas.

Doris *(more sharply than she intended)*: There's nothing in Las Vegas, Joe! *(She sits, trying to hold the edge of impatience inside* *of her, fishing desperately in her mind for something to say to her husband.)* Joe, I'm tired myself. I'd like to have a little peace. I'd like to know we live in a certain place and that a certain amount of money is coming in every week, so at least we know where we stand. I don't want a lot of money. I just don't want to have to carry a sick feeling in my stomach all the time that you're going to come home depressed and miserable. I don't want to listen to you turning around in bed all night long. I want to be able to go to sleep peacefully, knowing that you're also having a good night's sleep. I don't have much strength left, Joe. This kind of living is eating us up.

(Deeply exhausted, she rests her face in the palm of one hand. JOE stands silently. She has reached home with him. Finally he comes to her and gently takes her arm.)

Joe: It's all right, Doris, it's all right. Go to sleep.

Doris *(still hiding her face in her hand)*: You owe this to me, Joe.

Joe *(helps her from the chair)*: Go to sleep. I want to do a little thinking.

Doris: Joe, if I said anything that hurt you, it's because I'm all knocked out.

Joe *(helping her to the door)*: You didn't hurt me.

Doris: Let's go to bed. We'll get some sleep.

Joe: Go to sleep, Doris. You're all knocked out. I'm going to work out something. Don't worry. *(They stand now in the kitchen threshold, looking wearily at each other.)* I don't deserve you, Doris.

Doris: Come to bed, Joe.

Joe: In a couple of minutes.

(DORIS turns and shuffles out of view. JOE watches her disappearing form for a few moments. Then he turns and begins again the slow, measured pacing up and down the dining room. We stay with him for four or five lengths of the room. Fade out slowly.)

DISSOLVE TO:

Close-up of MARILYN's face. She is sleeping. We are in her bedroom, which is just off the living room. It is dark. MARILYN turns in her bed. Then she opens her eyes and awakens. She looks up. JOE *is standing beside her bed, looking down at her. She is up on her elbow immediately.*

Marilyn: Is something wrong, Pa?
Joe *(in a low voice)*: I wonder if I could talk to you for a minute, Marilyn.
Marilyn: Sure.
Joe: First let me finish. I need your five thousand dollars. I want to buy Louie Miles' land. It's the only piece of land I can get my hands on, do you understand? It's a piece of swamp. It's marsh. But it's the best I can get. I have to have land before I can manipulate. I know what it means to you, Marilyn, the five thousand dollars. I know you need it for your marriage. But you have to have faith in me. I'll give it back to you a thousand times over. Marilyn, I wouldn't ask you this, but I need it.
Marilyn: Sure, Pa. I'll make you out a check now. You can cash it in the morning.

(She starts to sit up. JOE stares at her, unbelieving. Then the tension breaks within him, and he begins to sob. He turns away from his daughter in shame and goes out into the living room, hiding his eyes in his hands, the sobs coming in hoarse, half-caught gasps. He walks aimlessly around the living room, hiding his eyes, crying uncontrollably. DORIS appears in the doorway of her room, watching him anxiously.)

Doris: What's the matter, Joe? You can't sleep?

Joe: Doris, I'll tell you what I've been thinking. I think I'm going to go away for a couple of days. I just called the station. I can get a train to St. Louis at four-forty-nine a.m. Then I catch a flyer for Las Vegas. *(He stands, begins to pace around, hands behind his back.)* At the convention last year in Atlantic City — a feller there from Las Vegas. He told me, Las Vegas is just booming. He says, houses are springing up overnight. A city jumping up out of the desert. Like Florida in the 1920s. Well, I think I'll take a look at this Las Vegas. Listen, a clever man can make himself a bundle. Then too, I might have a look in California, see what the situation on the coast is. Listen, I've heard wonderful things about the coast. Los Angeles, San Diego. I've got some friends in San

Diego. They told me: "Manx, any time you feel like switching your area of activity, there's plenty of room for you here."

Doris: Joe, come to bed.

(JOE comes to the table, leans intently across to his wife.)

Joe: Lady, I have a feeling Las Vegas is going to turn the trick. I was lying in bed thinking, and then, suddenly — like the burning bush — it came to me. It was like somebody spoke the thought aloud. "Go to Las Vegas." Why am I pushing pennies in Toledo? Well, let's pack up a couple of things for me and a toothbrush. *(He starts briskly past his wife for the kitchen door, but DORIS puts out a gentle hand on his forearm.)*

Doris: Joe . . . *(Her touch seems to crumble him. He turns to her, suddenly gaunt and broken.)*

Joe *(crying out)*: Doris! I gotta get outta this town!

Marilyn: Pa . . .

(He turns to her, still hiding his eyes.)

Joe *(brokenly)*: What did I ever give you? *(He sinks down onto a chair, cupping his face in both hands now. MARILYN moves slowly to him. DORIS returns to the bedroom.)*

Marilyn: Pa, look at me. Am I an unhappy girl? I'm happy. I love George. I love you. I love Mama. I got a responsible job. The boss is satisfied with me. That's what you gave me. I'll make you out the check.

(JOE has to shake his head a few times before he can answer.)

Joe: I don't want it. *(He rises weakly and starts for the kitchen door.)*

Marilyn: Pa . . .

Joe: Go to sleep, go to sleep . . . *(He goes into the kitchen, across it, and down the foyer to the door of his bedroom, opens it and goes in. DORIS is lying on her bed and turns to watch his entrance. He doesn't look at her. He goes to his bed, sits down. He is over his tears now and is just breathing heavily.)*

Joe *(mumbling)*: All right, all right. I'll take the job with Harry Gerber.

Doris: I didn't hear you, Joe.

Joe *(louder)*: I said, I'll take the job with Harry Gerber. At least, they'll have one honest building inspector. *(He lies back on the bed now, looking up at the ceiling.)* This was a crazy day, a crazy day. *(His eyes close and he dozes off.)*

FADE OUT

[1] **bantam:** a small and aggressive domestic fowl

A CLOSER LOOK

1. What job has Joe been offered? What is he trying to do instead? Why is he having trouble?

2. How does Joe see himself? How do his close friends and family see him? Who do you think has the most realistic view of Joe and his problems? Why?

3. What values in our society do you think influenced Joe's values? How do you think Chayefsky feels about these values? Give examples from the play. Do you think these are positive or negative values?

● Many poets complain about modern technology and how it has changed our society for the worse. Edward Field, however, defends one product of technology which we often take for granted — but which has made our lives richer.

Edward Field

THE TELEPHONE

My happiness depends on an electric appliance
And I do not mind giving it so much credit
With life in this city being what it is
Each person separated from friends
By a tangle of subways and buses
Yes, my telephone is my joy
It tells me that I am in the world and wanted
It rings and I am alerted to love or gossip
I go comb my hair which begins to sparkle
Without it I was like a bear in a cave
Drowsing through a shadowy winter
It rings and spring has come
I stretch and amble out into the sunshine
Hungry again as I pick up the receiver
For the human voice and the good news of friends.

"Well, guess who this is, writing to you after all these years!"

Norma Fox Mazer

DEAR BILL, REMEMBER ME?

● All of us have a few special friends — people we took to immediately; people who understood us inside and out; people who were there for us when nobody else was. Because these people mean so much, we hate to think we will ever lose them. But time passes, circumstances change — and people change. And in spite of the best intentions, close friends sometimes do drift apart.

Dear Bill,

Well, guess who this is, writing to you after all these years! Four years, to be exact. Today is Sunday, October 5, and the last time I saw you was on a Saturday in May. May 7, to be exact. Four years, five months, and two days, to be ex —

Dear Bill,

Remember me? It's been a long time since I saw you last. I figure (roughly speaking) about four years. Mucho water under the dam, as the saying goes. I wonder if you would recognize me now. I bet you wouldn't call me Bitsy anymore, even though I'm still not the world's tallest woman. But I've changed quite a bit (Nature, old boy, Nature) and so have certain other people around here that you used to know.

My mother, for instance, has gotten plump! What happened was, she decided to go back to work (driving a bus — cool, *n'est-ce pas?*[1]) and give up smoking at the same time. But she still *wants* to smoke like crazy, so instead she eats every chance she gets. You

113

should see the lunch bag she takes to work. Dad says everything except the kitchen sink goes into that bag. Dad is the same except he had to get glasses because he can't see little stuff like telephone numbers. And the other person you might be interested in hearing about, Judy — well, Judy is Judy. She's in college and, actually, I don't see that much of her anymore.

And what about you? Have you changed? I hope not. I always thought you were perfect, and I still th —

Dear Bill Old Chum,

This is Kathy speaking. Kathy Kalman. (Bitsy, to you.) Remember? Well, it's been a long time all right, Bill, plenty of water flowing under the dam, and thank goodness no one calls me Bitsy anymore. I never liked that name. Still, if we could have one of our good old long talks again, I wouldn't care what you called me — Kid, Bitsy, KK, Shorty — anything would be okay!

I've never been able to talk to anybody the way I talked to you. You listened to me, Bill. You took me seriously, me and my ideas, and even though you were so much older (seven years, remember?) you didn't look down on me, you didn't think it was beneath you to talk to me. You'd come over to see Judy, carrying a book under your arm, and you'd be early, as usual (you said it was a bad habit, that you had to get everywhere before everyone else), and if Judy wasn't ready, you'd say, "Come on, Bitsy, talk to me. Keep me company." Remember?

We'd go outside by the kitchen door and sit next to each other on top of the wooden steps leading from our back porch down to the yard, and we'd talk. Talk about *everything*. Sometimes, it would be about school. I told you once how Miss Fish, my gym teacher in fifth grade, had paddled one of the girls in front of everyone. I said to you that if she ever tried to do that to me, I would kill her. You didn't laugh. You didn't say, Oh you know you don't mean that, the way people do all the time. You put your arm around me, and you nodded, and said you knew how I felt.

Another time, you asked me, "If nobody hears the tree fall in the forest, has it fallen?" At first, I didn't know what you meant. It sounded so funny. But you were serious. You said philosophers had thought about this for thousands of years. "My own version, Bitsy, is: If I sit in my room and no one knows I'm there, how can *I* be sure I'm there?"

"But you are there, Bill."

"How do you know, Bitsy? How do I know? How do I know that I'm real, that I truly exist? What if it's all a dream? What if you're in my dream now, and I'm only part of your dream? How can you be sure?"

I wanted to laugh. I couldn't understand it. (I think I understand now.) You were always saying funny things, mocking things, mocking yourself, your nose especially.

Are you surprised how much I remember of things you said to me? ~~I remember other stuff, too, like the time you kis~~ I only wish I could remember everything, instead of just bits and pieces.

Well, Bill, reading back over this letter, I can see that I've really strayed off the beaten path, gone all around Robin Hood's barn, as my mother says. What I started out to say, what I wanted to write about was, Congrats, Old Chum, congrats. It's not every day a good old friend ups and —

Dear Bill,

Remember me? It's been one heck of a long —

Dear Bill,

Surprise! After all these years, you must be wondering why you're suddenly hearing from —

Dear Bill,

Just a brief note to say congratu —

Dear Bill,

All morning I've been trying to write you a letter and not getting very far. Every time I write something it sounds stupid to me and I give up. Do you remember me? Judy Kalman's ~~little~~ younger sister? I guess you remember Judy, all right. (Ha-ha.)

See what I mean about sounding stupid?!

The thing is, my head is full of stuff I want to tell you, and questions you haven't been around to answer for four years, and —

Look, I don't mean that as an accusation. Lots of people break their promises. I'm positive you had tons of other stuff on your mind. Anyway, if you want to be exact about it, I guess it wasn't actually a promise. I mean, you didn't say, *I promise* in so many words. You just said, "Bitsy, we'll keep in touch. Okay?"

115

And I said, "Yes."

I can see now that I was really a dope to think that was a promise and to go on waiting for years to hear from you. I guess you'd laugh if you could have seen me jump when the phone rang, or run for the mail every day after I heard you went away to college. My mother used to say, "Who do you think is going to write you, Kathy?" And I'd say, "Oh — nobody." And she'd say, "That's what I thought, because you don't write anybody." But I would have written you, Bill, if I'd known where. Would you have written me back?

Dear Bill,

This is ridiculous. I've been trying to write you a letter all morning and not getting anywhere. Well, this is it. I'm just getting on with this, writing whatever comes into my head, and the heck with it!

One thing I've been dying to tell you is that we read *Cyrano* in English. And guess who it made me think of right away! I love Cyrano, Bill. I adore him. "A great nose indicates a great man — genial, courteous, intellectual, virile, courageous . . . " Cyrano de Bill!

All those jokes about your nose. You said your nose was so big it got in the way of your seeing straight. (It never occurred to me then that you might be self-conscious. Well, you shouldn't have been. Big nose or not, I thought you were terrific-looking.) You used to intone, *Who knows what evil lurks in this nose? The Nose knows.* You'd put on your Fiendish Murderer face. And remember Mr. P.R.O. Biz Kiss, the Inquiring Reporter? "Where my nose goes, I follow, sniffing out the truth wherever it may lead." Mr. P.R.O. Biz Kiss could flare his nostrils and twitch his nose like a rabbit at the same time. Very talented, he was!

Bill — remember the time I sneaked up on you and Judy? That was a kid-sister, bratty kind of thing to do. I always wanted to explain to you about that, because I felt you were disappointed in me. (Were you?) That day, I was coming home from school, thinking how strange things were. I don't know why it happened just then, but all of a sudden that day, I had a different view of everything. Cars looked weird to me, and the clothes people wore, sidewalks, houses. As if everything was unreal. I kept thinking, Where did all this come from? How did it all get here? I had a feeling that someone could just peel off our whole city from the face of the earth like some cruddy scab. I suppose, for the first time, I was really thinking about things the way you always did, not just accepting everything — here I am, here's my parents and Judy, here's our house, school, the stores, and here it belongs. Instead, I had this dizzy feeling of it all being — well, superficial, not really *rooted*.

It was spring, I remember, and the city maintenance crew had just come along and filled up the potholes in our street and suddenly it terrified me that beneath the smooth, seemingly solid road was just a lot of dirt. Everything was so flimsy, everything I'd ever thought of as solid and unmovable. Cars and trucks traveled over roads, and houses stood on foundations, but I felt that in a moment it could all crumple like paper.

And then I came to our house — we were living upstairs on Second Street then, but we've moved, did you know that? — and as I started up the stairs, I was testing every step because I still had that queer, scary feeling of everything being impermanent. And suddenly I knew that you and Judy were in our living room, that you were all alone in the house.

As soon as I thought that, I started creeping quietly up the stairs. I didn't know why, but thinking about you and Judy made me forget the other sickening, frightening thoughts I'd been having. I stopped feeling dizzy and went on quietly, as quietly as I could, up the stairs. I didn't know what I was going to do. I really and truly didn't know, didn't think to myself that I was doing something sneaky or wrong.

I just kept creeping up, opened the door as quietly as I could, and walked quietly into the living room. And just as I'd somehow known I'd find you, you both were there, on the couch together.

Judy saw me first. "Get out!" she yelled. The two of you fell apart, sort of jumped up or scrambled off the couch. I couldn't move. I felt — I don't know how to say it — hurt, I guess. Isn't that stupid? I mean, I *knew* what I was going to see. I'd had sort of a pre-vision. And yet, I just felt so hurt, so bad.

"You little spy," Judy said. Her cheeks were all red, shiny, as if she had a fever. "Spy! Sneak!" I shook my head. I wanted to explain, to say something, but nothing would come out.

I could hear my heart, or feel it, I wasn't sure which, making this hollow sound inside me. I'd never heard it before and it scared me terribly. I thought, *I'm going to die right now. Because I did this.* And still, all I could do was stand there and shake my head. I think I was waiting for you to say something. It was like I was in a spell and only you could break it. You were looking at me, your blond hair sticking out every which way, and your eyes sad, I thought, because I'd done something to hurt you.

And then — isn't it funny, queer, I mean — then I can't remember what happened next. I don't remember leaving the room or anything like that. The next thing I remember is Judy following me around offering me money not to tell Mom. I hated her for that, for thinking I'd betray her or you. And I guess she hated me, figuring I was holding it over her head. But torture wouldn't have made me reveal one single tiny fraction of what I'd seen. (One day I locked myself in the bathroom, poked a needle into my thumb four times, one time for each letter of your name, and with each drop of blood swore myself to silence.)

Are you laughing your head off, Bill? I wouldn't blame you, but I hope not. I hope you can understand that I was eleven and you were eighteen and I thought you were very special. Once you said to me, "Bitsy, when you grow up, you're going to drive some guy crazy." That was the time you kissed me. I guess you hardly remember it, since it wasn't a real kiss. I mean, it wasn't on the mouth or anything. You kind of stroked my hair and then you kissed me on the cheek. And you said, "You better be sure and let me know when you're sixteen. I want to be there when that time comes."

Well, I'm fifteen and one-half now, Bill, almost there, but I guess it doesn't matter anymore. I mean, I read about you and Lucille Lacy Heller Marginy in the newspaper —

Dear Bill,

This is a letter from an old friend who will probably remain nameless, but who wants to speak frankly to you concerning the Marginy woman. 1. She is thirty years old. 2. She has been married before. 3. She has two kids who are both spoiled. I know this for a fact because ~~Randy Southworth~~ a trusted friend has been Mrs. Marginy's baby-sitter twice when she couldn't get her regular sitter, and this friend could do nothing whatsoever with the children. 4. She is too old for —

Dear Bill,

It's been quite a few years since I saw you last. Over four years, since it was in May four years ago that you and my sister, Judy,

118

"Get out!"

broke up. I happened to be there at the time it happened. Do you remember?

We were all out riding in your car, your old jalopy you called Spirit of Syracuse. I think Judy was mad at you because you let me come along.

I kept wishing you'd say, "Bitsy, come on up in front with us." Over and over I imagined you saying, "Move over, Judy, make room for Bitsy." But I didn't say anything. I was conscious of trying not to butt in, not to make too much of a pest of myself. I was just glad to go anyplace with you and Judy. I never thought Judy was nice enough to you, and I told myself you only liked her because she was so pretty. (Mom and Dad have noticed that my CQ — clumsy quotient — goes up when Judy comes home, and they've tried to straighten me out — or up — by telling me I have no need to be jealous just because Judy is prettier and basically more successful in school.) I'm not jealous, truly. I like who I am. I've liked who I am ever since I knew you, Bill, because you liked me. But that didn't stop me from having spiteful eleven-year-old thoughts about my sister.

I was telling myself my pretty sister looked like a Talking Barbie

"Come on, Judy, let's get in the car."

and, sitting behind her, I decided I could see a short piece of cord sticking out of her back. Pull the cord and Talking Barbie says, "Hello! I am Talking Barbie. I am taking a ride with Talking Ken. Talking Ken and I are having fun. Talking Ken and I are going to swim. Watch me swim in my sexy bikini."

I got myself all wrapped up, concentrating really hard on that idea. Mind over matter. Maybe if I concentrated superhard I could really turn Judy into Talking Barbie and then you and I would pack her up and ship her back to the Barbie factory to find Malibu Barbie, Talking Francie, and Growing Barbie.

When I finally tuned in on you and Judy again, you were fighting. That kind of low-voice fighting, where people still sound polite, and you can't figure out what's going on. Judy was saying, "You're supersensitive, Bill, about being poor, I never meant it that way."

And you said, "Supersensitive, my eye."

That was the end of the low voices. You told her that was ridiculous. And she said you'd better stop calling her names. And you said she was being juvenile.

"Okay!" she said. "Okay. Stop the car! I want to get out."

You wouldn't stop. You said that was silly and immature, you weren't going to let her walk ten miles back to the city.

"That's my decision, not yours," Judy said.

Suddenly you stopped the car. And she got out. For about two seconds, I was joyful, waiting for you to drive off so I could leap over the back seat and sit next to you, right where Judy had been sitting. Then she remembered me. "Okay, Bitsy, out! We're walking!"

And we walked. You drove away. I was furious with her because it was a hot day, the road stunk of carbon monoxide fumes from the cars whizzing by, and besides all that, I was barefoot.

You doubled back for us. We'd been walking for about twenty minutes, and I was so relieved. But Judy was too proud to get into the car without an apology. You said you had nothing to apologize for and that she was acting even more ridiculous and immature than you had thought her capable of acting.

I think I remember all that, practically word for word, because I was really torn. I was rooting for you, and yet I couldn't help being on my sister's side, too, mad as I was at her. "Come on, Judy, let's get in the car," I said. You were leaning on the window, your arms crossed. You winked at me.

"Come on, Judy," you said, "listen to Bitsy."

"Forget it." Judy started walking again. "Forget it, forget it, just *forget* it," she said, passing right by you.

"I'll forget it, all right," you said. "I'll forget you. That won't be too hard!" And you drove away, then suddenly backed up, stuck your head out the window and called, "Bitsy, we'll keep in touch. Okay?"

I said, "Yes!" And then you were really gone.

I caught up with Judy. We walked along for a while, then she started talking about you. How arrogant you were. You were so sure you were brighter, smarter, more intellectual than anyone. How you were always correcting her. "He thinks he's so much, and he's nothing," she said. "He doesn't even have a decent family!"

"Yes, he does." I was getting crosser and crosser with Judy. I knew you came from a poor family, that your father drove a beat-up truck and went around picking up stuff from other people's garbage and throwouts. And once I saw you downtown with your mother and she was wearing a long brown skirt and sneakers with her toes sticking out. But I thought Judy was being stupid, and I told her.

"Oh, now you're starting in on me," she said. And she started to cry. "You think he's so perfect, so wonderful. Oh, I know, don't think I don't know."

It's queer how it's all coming back to me now as I'm writing this. I can smell the tar on the road that day, it was so hot, a hot day in May, and I can almost feel all over again the gravel under my bare feet, and then hear Judy saying, "He's impossible, impossible, you can't say anything to him!"

And then the next thing I remember is being in my room, it's night, it's cool, and it's raining outside. And I'm thinking to myself, *Well, even if Judy and Bill don't get together again, I'll still get to see him.*

But I never did. I can't believe it sometimes. You're so real to me, Bill. I can *see* you perfectly clearly in my mind, and yet — are you there, Bill? If I don't actually see you, do you still exist?

Dear Bill,

Glancing through the newspaper the other day, I noticed the announcement of your marriage to Lucille Lacy Heller Marginy, and I want to congratulate you —

Dear Bill,

A funny thing happened last week. I was out driving with my girlfriend, Randy, and we were on Rock Cut Road and suddenly we passed your house, a little pink house sitting back there behind that old cemetery, with your father's truck parked nearby, ~~and all that old junk in the yard,~~ and all of a sudden I remembered that you once took me to your house. I met your brother, Tim, and your sister, Nancy. And we had gingersnaps and milk. But the funny thing is that I hadn't even been on Rock Cut Road in years, and then, the way coincidences happen, yesterday my mother saw the announcement of your marriage in the newspaper. "Mr. and Mrs. Clarence Heller of Woodchuck Hill Road, DeWitt, announce the marriage of their daughter, Lucille Lacy Heller Marginy, to William Youngman, Jr., of Rock Cut Road, Jamesville."

My mother said, "Do you remember Judy's old boyfriend, Kathy? Bill Youngman?"

So I said, "Sure." And I laughed because she could even ask me such a question. Then she passed the newspaper over to me.

And she said, "Well, it's quite a jump from Rock Cut Road to Woodchuck Hill Road. I don't think there's a house out there on

Woodchuck Hill Road under fifty thousand.''

Oh, why am I saying all this to you? It sounds so snobby and stupid! Bill, I just can't get this letter to you right. I want to say so many things, and it's all coming out wrong. It sounds like I care one way or the other where you were born, and I don't. I don't! I —

Dear Bill,

Why did you do it? I keep wondering, why? Are you in love with her? But she's so old. And you said to me, You better let me know when you're sixteen, I want to be there. You said it, and I believed you, Bill! I'm growing up, I'm nearly sixteen, I'm nearly there, if only you'd waited another year!

Bill, why didn't you write me even once? Just a postcard would have been okay. Or a call to say, Hello, how are you, Bitsy, what are you doing, what are you thinking?

If I told you all the times I made up conversations you and I could have — if you knew all the letters I've wanted to write you. What if I had written them? Would you have done it? Married her? Oh, I know I'm being an absolute jerk, but, Bill —

Dear Bill,

I love you and have ever since I knew you. I don't think I'll ever forget you or stop lov —

Dear Bill,

The other day I noticed an announcement of your marriage in the newspaper. We were friends a long time ago, and so I want to wish you the best of everything.

Peace.

Kathy (Bitsy) Kalman

[1] *n'est-ce pas:* isn't it?

A CLOSER LOOK

1. How did Bitsy first get to know Bill?

2. Why does Bitsy write so many versions of this letter?

3. Think of some friend you used to have who isn't part of your life anymore. What did you gain from knowing this person?

"Just creeps in, has some food, then flits away."

James Herriot

A KITTEN
FOR MRS. AINSWORTH

- James Herriot is one of the world's best-loved story writers, but he has another career as well — as a veterinarian in the countryside of Yorkshire, in northern England. Most of his stories, in fact, are drawn from his experience as a vet. In his work, he has seen every different kind of relationship there is between an animal and a human being — but this one touched him more than most.

MY STRONGEST MEMORY OF CHRISTMAS WILL always be bound up with a certain little cat. I first saw her when I was called to see one of Mrs. Ainsworth's dogs. I looked in some surprise at the furry black creature sitting before the fire.

"I didn't know you had a cat," I said.

The lady smiled. "We haven't. This is Debbie."

"Debbie?"

"Yes, at least that's what we call her. She's a stray. Comes here two or three times a week and we give her some food. I don't know where she lives but I believe she spends a lot of her time around one of the farms along the road."

"Do you ever get the feeling that she wants to stay with you?"

"No." Mrs. Ainsworth shook her head. "She's a timid little thing. Just creeps in, has some food, then flits away. There's something so appealing about her, but she doesn't seem to want to let me or anybody into her life."

I looked at the little cat. "But she just isn't having food today."

"That's right. It's a funny thing but every now and again she slips through here into the lounge and sits by the fire for a few minutes. It's as though she was giving herself a treat."

"Yes . . . I see what you mean." There was no doubt there was something unusual in the attitude of the little animal. She was sitting bolt upright on the thick rug which lay before the fireplace. The coals glowed and flamed. She made no effort to curl up or wash herself or do anything other than gaze quietly ahead. And there was something in the dusty black of her coat, the half-wild scrawny look of her, that gave me a clue. This was a special event in her life, a rare and wonderful thing. She was lapping up a comfort undreamed of in her daily existence.

As I watched, she turned, crept soundlessly from the room, and was gone.

"That's always the way with Debbie," Mrs. Ainsworth laughed. "She never stays more than ten minutes or so, then she's off."

Mrs. Ainsworth was a plumpish, pleasant-faced woman in her forties. She was the kind of client veterinary surgeons dream of; well off, generous, and the owner of three Basset hounds. It only needed the usual mournful expressions of one of the dogs to deepen a little and I was sent for post-haste.[1] Today one of the Bassets had raised its paw and scratched its ear a couple of times. That was enough to send its mistress running to the phone in great alarm.

My visits to the Ainsworth home were frequent but undemanding. I had ample opportunity to look out for the little cat which had intrigued me. On one occasion I spotted her nibbling daintily from a saucer at the kitchen door. As I watched, she turned and almost floated on light footsteps into the hall, then through the lounge door.

The three Bassets were already in residence, draped snoring on the fireside rug. They seemed to be used to Debbie, because two of them sniffed her in a bored manner and the third merely cocked a sleepy eye at her before flopping back on the rich carpet.

Debbie sat among them in her usual posture: upright, intent, gazing absorbedly into the glowing coals. This time I tried to make friends with her. I approached her carefully, but she leaned away as I stretched out my hand. However, by patient wheedling[2] and soft talk I managed to touch her and gently stroked her cheek with one finger. There was a moment when she responded by putting her head on one side and rubbing back against my hand, but soon she was ready to leave. Once outside the house she darted quickly along the

126

road, then through a gap in a hedge. The last I saw was the little black figure flitting over the rain-swept grass of a field.

"I wonder where she goes," I murmured half to myself.

Mrs. Ainsworth appeared at my elbow. "That's something we've never been able to find out."

It must have been nearly three months before I heard from Mrs. Ainsworth.

It was Christmas morning and she was apologetic. "Mr. Herriot, I'm so sorry to bother you today of all days. I should think you want a rest at Christmas like anybody else." But her natural politeness could not hide the distress in her voice.

"Please don't worry about that," I said. "Which one is it this time?"

"It's not one of the dogs. It's . . . Debbie."

"Debbie? She's at your house now?"

"Yes . . . but there's something wrong. Please come quickly."

I drove through the marketplace of Darrowby on Christmas Day. The snow lay thick on the cobbles and hung from the eaves of roofs. The shops were closed. The colored lights of the Christmas trees winked at the windows of the clustering houses. They were warmly inviting against the cold white bulk of the fells[3] behind.

Mrs. Ainsworth's home was lavishly decorated with tinsel and holly. Rows of drinks stood on the sideboard. The rich aroma of turkey and sage and onion stuffing floated through to the lounge.

Debbie was there all right, but this time everything was different. She wasn't sitting upright in her usual position. She was stretched quite motionless on her side, and huddled close to her lay a tiny black kitten.

I looked down in bewilderment. "What's happened here?"

"It's the strangest thing," Mrs. Ainsworth replied. "I hadn't seen her for several weeks, then she came in about two hours ago — sort of staggered into the kitchen, and she was carrying the kitten in her mouth. She took it through to the lounge and laid it on the rug. At first I was amused. But I could see all was not well because she sat as she usually does, but for a long time — over an hour — then she lay down like this and she hasn't moved."

I knelt on the rug and passed my hand over Debbie's neck and ribs. She was thinner than ever. Her fur was dirty and mud-caked. She did not resist as I gently opened her mouth. The tongue and

"The tiny mouth opened in a soundless miaow."

mucous membranes were abnormally pale. The lips were ice-cold against my fingers. When I pulled down her eyelid and saw the dead white conjunctiva, a knell[4] sounded in my mind.

I examined the abdomen with a grim certainty as to what I would find. There was no surprise, only a dull sadness as my fingers closed around a hard mass deep among the organs. Massive lymphosarcoma. Terminal[5] and hopeless. I put my stethoscope on her heart and listened to the increasingly faint, rapid beat. Then I straightened up and sat on the rug, looking sightlessly into the fireplace, feeling the warmth of the flames on my face.

Mrs. Ainsworth's voice seemed to come from afar. "Is she ill, Mr. Herriot?"

I hesitated. "Yes, I'm afraid so. She has a fatal growth." I stood up. "There's absolutely nothing I can do. I'm sorry."

"Oh!" Her hand went to her mouth and she looked at me wide-eyed. When at last she spoke her voice trembled. "Well, you must put her to sleep immediately. It's the only thing to do. We can't let her suffer."

"Mrs. Ainsworth," I said. "There's no need. She's dying now — in a coma — far beyond suffering."

She turned quickly away from me. She was very still as she fought with her emotions. Then she gave up the struggle and dropped on her knees beside Debbie.

"Oh, poor little thing!" she sobbed, and stroked the cat's head again and again as the tears fell unchecked on the matted fur. "What she must have come through. I feel I ought to have done more for her."

For a few moments I was silent, feeling her sorrow, so out of place among the bright seasonal colors of this festive room. Then I spoke gently.

"Nobody could have done more than you," I said. "Nobody could have been kinder."

"But I'd have kept her here — in comfort. It must have been terrible out there in the cold when she was so desperately ill — I daren't think about it. And having kittens, too — I . . . I wonder how many she did have?"

I shrugged. "I don't suppose we'll ever know. Maybe just this one. It happens sometimes. And she brought it to you, didn't she?"

"Yes . . . that's right . . . she did . . . she did." Mrs. Ainsworth reached out and lifted the bedraggled black morsel. She smoothed her finger along the muddy fur. The tiny mouth opened in a soundless miaow.

"Isn't it strange? She was dying and she brought her kitten here. And on Christmas Day."

I bent and put my hand on Debbie's heart. There was no beat.

I looked up. "I'm afraid she's gone." I lifted the small body, almost feather-light, wrapped it in the sheet which had been spread on the rug, and took it out to the car.

When I came back Mrs. Ainsworth was still stroking the kitten. The tears had dried on her cheeks and she was bright-eyed as she looked at me.

"I've never had a cat before," she said.

I smiled. "Well, it looks as though you've got one now."

---

[1] **post-haste:** in a great hurry
[2] **wheedling:** flattery
[3] **fells:** bare hills; high rocky ground
[4] **knell:** the sound of a bell that rings for the dead or dying
[5] **terminal:** at the end; resulting in death

A CLOSER LOOK

1. How do you think Debbie lived from day to day? Why do you think she came to Mrs. Ainsworth in the end?

2. Why do you think Herriot has a special interest in this cat? How is Debbie different from the rest of the Ainsworth household?

3. Why do you think Mrs. Ainsworth takes the kitten? What makes people become close to their animals?

● Wouldn't it be wonderful to go back in time and erase all the mistakes we made the first time around! If only we could all start again, and do things differently!

David Huddle

ICICLE

I smacked you in the mouth for no good reason
except that the icicle had broken off
so easily and that it felt like a club
in my hand, and so I swung it, the soft
pad of your lower lip sprouting a drop,
then gushing a trail onto the snow even
though we both squeezed the place with our fingers.
I'd give a lot not to be the swinger
of that icicle. I'd like another
morning just like that, cold, windy, and bright
as Russia, your glasses fogging up, your face
turning to me again. I tell you I might
help both our lives by changing that act to this,
by handing you the ice, a gift, my brother.

"There is a strange communion between a boy and a dog."

Marjorie Kinnan Rawlings

A MOTHER IN MANNVILLE

● Why do two people sometimes feel that they belong to each other? Family ties, romantic love, or friendship between equals form the basis for most relationships. But human beings can forge other ties, too — based on mutual respect. Marjorie Kinnan Rawlings often wrote with admiration of courageous and independent spirits she had met. The subject of this autobiographical story, however, is a special bond that grows between a lonely boy and the woman who befriends him.

THE ORPHANAGE IS HIGH IN THE CAROLINA MOUN-tains. Sometimes in winter the snowdrifts are so deep that the institution is cut off from the village below, from the world. Fog hides the mountain peaks, the snow swirls down the valleys, and a wind blows so bitterly that the orphanage boys who take the milk twice daily to the baby cottage reach the door with fingers stiff in an agony of numbness.

"Or when we carry trays from the cookhouse for the ones that are sick," Jerry said, "we get our faces frostbit, because we can't put our hands over them. I have gloves," he added. "Some of the boys don't have any."

He liked the late spring, he said. The rhododendron was in bloom, a carpet of color, across the mountainsides, soft as the May winds that stirred the hemlocks. He called it laurel.

"It's pretty when the laurel blooms," he said. "Some of it's pink and some of it's white."

I was there in autumn. I wanted quiet, isolation, to do some troublesome writing. I wanted mountain air to blow out the malaria

133

"I saw him going up over the hill in the twilight."

from too long a time in the subtropics. I was homesick, too, for the flaming of maples in October, and for corn shocks and pumpkins and black-walnut trees and the lift of hills. I found them all, living in a cabin that belonged to the orphanage, half a mile beyond the orphanage farm. When I took the cabin, I asked for a boy or man to come and chop wood for the fireplace. The first few days were warm. I found that wood I needed about the cabin. No one came, and I forgot the order.

I looked up from my typewriter one late afternoon, a little startled. A boy stood at the door, and my pointer dog, my companion, was at his side and had not barked to warn me. The boy was probably twelve years old, but undersized. He wore overalls and a torn shirt, and was barefooted.

He said, "I can chop some wood today."

I said, "But I have a boy coming from the orphanage."

"I'm the boy."

"You? But you're small."

"Size don't matter, chopping wood," he said. "Some of the big boys don't chop good. I've been chopping wood at the orphanage a long time."

I visualized mangled and inadequate branches for my fires. I was well into my work and not inclined to conversation. I was a little blunt.

"Very well. There's the ax. Go ahead and see what you can do."

I went back to work, closing the door. At first the sound of the boy dragging brush annoyed me. Then he began to chop. The blows were rhythmic and steady, and shortly I had forgotten him. The sound was no more of an interruption than a consistent rain. I suppose an hour and a half passed, for when I stopped and stretched, and heard the boy's steps on the cabin stoop, the sun was dropping behind the farthest mountain, and the valleys were purple with something deeper than the asters.

The boy said, "I have to go to supper now. I can come again tomorrow evening."

I said, "I'll pay you now for what you've done," thinking I should probably have to insist on an older boy. "Ten cents an hour?"

"Anything is all right."

We went together back of the cabin. An astonishing amount of solid wood had been cut. There were cherry logs and heavy roots of rhododendron, and blocks from the waste pine and oak left from the building of the cabin.

"But you've done as much as a man," I said. "This is a splendid pile."

I looked at him, actually, for the first time. His hair was the color of the shocks, and his eyes, very direct, were like the mountain sky when rain is pending — gray, with a showing of that miraculous blue. As I spoke a light came over him, as though the setting sun had touched him with the same suffused[1] glory with which it touched the mountains. I gave him a quarter.

"You may come tomorrow," I said, "and thank you very much."

He looked at me, and at the coin, and seemed to want to speak, but could not, and turned away.

"I'll split the kindling tomorrow," he said over his thin ragged shoulder. "You'll need kindling and medium wood and logs and backlogs."

At daylight I was half awakened by the sound of chopping. Again it was so even in texture that I went back to sleep. When I left my bed in the cool morning, the boy had come and gone, and a stack of

135

kindling was neat against the cabin wall. He came again after school in the afternoon and worked until time to return to the orphanage. His name was Jerry; he was twelve years old, and he had been at the orphanage since he was four. I could picture him at four, with the same grave gray-blue eyes and the same — independence? No, the word that comes to me is "integrity."[2]

The word means something very special to me, and the quality for which I use it is a rare one. My father had it — there is another of whom I am almost sure — but almost no man of my acquaintance possesses it with the clarity, the purity, the simplicity of a mountain stream. But the boy Jerry had it. It is bedded on courage, but it is more than brave. It is honest, but it is more than honesty. The ax handle broke one day. Jerry said the woodshop at the orphanage would repair it. I brought money to pay for the job and he refused it.

"I'll pay for it," he said. "I broke it. I brought the ax down careless."

"But no one hits accurately every time," I told him. "The fault was in the wood of the handle. I'll see the man from whom I bought it."

It was only then that he would take the money. He was standing back of his own carelessness. He was a free-will agent and he chose to do careful work, and if he failed, he took the responsibility without subterfuge.[3]

And he did for me the unnecessary thing, the gracious thing, that we find done only by the great of heart. Things no training can teach, for they are done on the instant, with no predicated experience. He found a cubbyhole beside the fireplace that I had not noticed. There, of his own accord, he put kindling and "medium" wood, so that I might always have dry fire material ready in case of sudden wet weather. A stone was loose in the rough walk to the cabin. He dug a deeper hole and steadied it, although he came, himself, by a shortcut over the bank. I found that when I tried to return his thoughtfulness with such things as candy and apples, he was wordless. "Thank you" was, perhaps, an expression for which he had had no use, for his courtesy was instinctive. He only looked at the gift and at me, and a curtain lifted, so that I saw deep into the clear well of his eyes, and gratitude was there, and affection, soft over the firm granite of his character.

He made simple excuses to come and sit with me. I could no more have turned him away than if he had been physically hungry. I suggested once that the best time for us to visit was just before supper, when I left off my writing. After that, he waited always until my typewriter had been some time quiet. One day I worked until nearly dark. I went outside the cabin, having forgotten him. I saw him going up over the hill in the twilight toward the orphanage. When I sat down on my stoop, a place was warm from his body where he had been sitting.

He became intimate, of course, with my pointer, Pat. There is a strange communion between a boy and a dog. Perhaps they possess the same singleness of spirit, the same kind of wisdom. It is difficult to explain, but it exists. When I went across the state for a weekend I left the dog in Jerry's charge. I gave him the dog whistle and the key to the cabin, and left sufficient food. He was to come two or three times a day and let out the dog, and feed and exercise him. I should return Sunday night, and Jerry would take out the dog for the last time Sunday afternoon and then leave the key under an agreed hiding place.

My return was belated[4] and fog filled the mountain passes so treacherously that I dared not drive at night. The fog held the next morning, and it was Monday noon before I reached the cabin. The dog had been fed and cared for that morning. Jerry came early in the afternoon, anxious.

"The superintendent said nobody would drive in the fog," he said. "I came just before bedtime last night and you hadn't come. So I brought Pat some of my breakfast this morning. I wouldn't have let anything happen to him."

"I was sure of that. I didn't worry."

"When I heard about the fog, I thought you'd know."

He was needed for work at the orphanage and he had to return at once. I gave him a dollar in payment, and he looked at it and went away. But that night he came in the darkness and knocked at the door.

"Come in, Jerry," I said, "if you're allowed to be away this late."

"I told maybe a story," he said. "I told them I thought you would want to see me."

"That's true," I assured him, and I saw his relief. "I want to hear about how you managed with the dog."

He sat by the fire with me, with no other light, and told me of their two days together. The dog lay close to him, and found a comfort there that I did not have for him. And it seemed to me that being with my dog, and caring for him, had brought the boy and me, too, together, so that he felt that he belonged to me as well as to the animal.

"He stayed right with me," he told me, "except when he ran in the laurel. He likes the laurel. I took him up over the hill and we both ran fast. There was a place where the grass was high and I lay down in it and hid. I could hear Pat hunting for me. He found my trail and he barked. When he found me, he acted crazy, and he ran around and around me, in circles."

We watched the flames.

"That's an apple log," he said. "It burns the prettiest of any wood."

We were very close.

He was suddenly impelled to speak of things he had not spoken of before, nor had I cared to ask him.

"You look a little bit like my mother," he said. "Especially in the dark, by the fire."

"But you were only four, Jerry, when you came here. You have remembered how she looked, all these years?"

"My mother lives in Mannville," he said.

For a moment, finding that he had a mother shocked me as greatly as anything in my life has ever done, and I did not know why it disturbed me. Then I understood my distress. I was filled with a passionate resentment that any woman should go away and leave her son. A fresh anger added itself. A son like this one — the orphanage was a wholesome place, the executives were kind, good people. The food was more than adequate, the boys were healthy, a ragged shirt was no hardship, nor the doing of clean labor. Granted, perhaps, that the boy felt no lack, what about the mother? At four he would have looked the same as now. Nothing, I thought, nothing in life could change those eyes. His quality must be apparent to an idiot, a fool. I burned with questions I could not ask. In any, I was afraid, there would be pain.

"Have you seen her, Jerry — lately?"

"I see her every summer. She sends for me."

I wanted to cry out. "Why are you not with her? How can she let you go away again?"

He said, "She comes up here from Mannville whenever she can. She doesn't have a job now."

"He would lie on the floor in front of the fire."

His face shone in the firelight.

"She wanted to give me a puppy, but they can't let any one boy keep a puppy. You remember the suit I had on last Sunday?" He was plainly proud. "She sent me that for Christmas. The Christmas before that" — he drew a long breath, savoring the memory — "she sent me a pair of skates."

"Roller skates?"

My mind was busy, making pictures of her, trying to understand her. She had not, then, entirely deserted or forgotten him. But why, then — I thought, "But I must not condemn her without knowing."

"Roller skates. I let the other boys use them. They're always borrowing them. But they're careful of them."

What circumstances other than poverty —

"I'm going to take the dollar you gave me for taking care of Pat," he said, "and buy her a pair of gloves."

I could only say, "That will be nice. Do you know her size?"

"I think it's eight and a half," he said.

He looked at my hands.

"Do you wear eight and a half?" he asked.

"No. I wear a smaller size, a six."

"Oh! Then I guess her hands are bigger than yours."

I hated her. Poverty or no, there was other food than bread, and the soul could starve as quickly as the body. He was taking his dollar to buy gloves for her big stupid hands, and she lived away from him, in Mannville, and contented herself with sending him skates.

"She likes white gloves," he said. "Do you think I can get them for a dollar?"

"I think so," I said.

I decided that I should not leave the mountains without seeing her and knowing for myself why she had done this thing.

The human mind scatters its interests as though made of thistledown, and every wind stirs and moves it. I finished my work. It did not please me, and I gave my thoughts to another field. I should need some Mexican material.

I made arrangements to close my Florida place. Mexico immediately, and doing the writing there, if conditions were favorable. Then, Alaska with my brother. After that, heaven knew what or where.

I did not take time to go to Mannville to see Jerry's mother, nor even to talk with the orphanage officials about her. I was a trifle abstracted[5] about the boy, because of my work and plans. And after my first fury at her — we did not speak of her again — his having a mother, any sort at all, not far away, in Mannville, relieved me of the ache I had had about him. He did not question the anomalous[6] relation. He was not lonely. It was none of my concern.

He came every day and cut my wood and did small helpful favors and stayed to talk. The days had become cold, and often I let him come inside the cabin. He would lie on the floor in front of the fire, with one arm across the pointer, and they would both doze and wait quietly for me. Other days they ran with a common ecstasy through the laurel, and since the asters were now gone, he brought me back vermillion[7] maple leaves, and chestnut boughs dripping with imperial yellow. I was ready to go.

I said to him, "You have been my good friend, Jerry. I shall often think of you and miss you. Pat will miss you, too. I am leaving tomorrow."

He did not answer. When he went away, I remember that a new moon hung over the mountains, and I watched him go in silence up the hill. I expected him the next day, but he did not come. The details of packing my personal belongings, loading my car, arranging the bed over the seat, where the dog would ride, occupied me until late in the day. I closed the cabin and started the car, noticing that the sun was in the west and I should do well to be out of the mountains by nightfall. I stopped by the orphanage and left the cabin key and money for my light bill with Miss Clark.

"And will you call Jerry for me to say good-bye to him?"

"I don't know where he is," she said. "I'm afraid he's not well. He didn't eat his dinner this noon. One of the boys saw him going over the hill into the laurel. He was supposed to fire the boiler this afternoon. It's not like him; he's unusually reliable."

I was almost relieved, for I knew I should never see him again, and it would be easier not to say good-bye to him.

I said, "I wanted to talk with you about his mother — why he's here — but I'm in more of a hurry than I expected to be. It's out of the question for me to see her now. But here's some money I'd like to leave with you to buy things for him at Christmas and on his birthday. It will be better than for me to try to send him things. I could so easily duplicate — skates, for instance."

She blinked her honest spinster's eyes.

"There's not much use for skates here," she said.

Her stupidity annoyed me.

"What I mean," I said, "is that I don't want to duplicate things his mother sends him. I might have chosen skates if I didn't know she had already given them to him."

"I don't understand," she said. "He has no mother. He has no skates."

[1] **suffused:** spread over or through as with liquid or light
[2] **integrity:** honesty
[3] **subterfuge:** evasion; deception
[4] **belated:** delayed
[5] **abstracted:** absentminded; detached; preoccupied
[6] **anomalous:** not in keeping with the usual rule or method
[7] **vermillion:** bright red or red-orange

A CLOSER LOOK

1. Why does the writer admire Jerry?

2. How does the writer feel about Jerry's mother?

3. What do you think will happen to Jerry in the future?

Hugh Prather

NOTES TO MYSELF: RELATIONSHIPS

● Like many aspiring writers, Prather kept a journal in which he jotted down observations on life. As it turned out, this journal was more interesting than the novel he was trying to write, so he published the journal instead, and it became a best-seller. In reflecting on his own life, Prather focused on problems that many people probably share with him. Like all of us, he was always learning new things about how to get along with other people.

"You ought to" means "I want you to," so why not say so?

As long as I'm giving you things I don't have to notice you.

I can get along with people a lot better if I realize that no one ever feels exactly the same about me or anyone else from one moment to the next. And, likewise, it is self-destructive to believe *I* must love anyone all of the time.

I am afraid of your silence because of what it could mean. I suspect your silence of meaning you are getting bored or losing interest or making up your own mind about me without my guidance. I believe that as long as I keep you talking I can know what you are thinking. But silence can also mean confidence. And mutual respect. Silence can mean live and let live: the appreciation that I am I and you are you. This silence is an affirmation that we are already together — as two people. Words can mean that I want to make you into a friend and silence can mean that I accept your already being one.

There is something about compliments that scares me. Part of the reason may be that I am afraid of getting something that can subsequently be taken away. I put myself in the hands of this other person if I let my emotions lean on his statement. Another reason: I am being put on the spot and now must watch my actions to keep him thinking this way about me. Another: There is a part of me that knows I am not as good as his compliment implies. Another: I have often been insincere when saying similar things.

A CLOSER LOOK

1. Which of these notes try to understand how other people behave? Which ones examine how the author himself feels and behaves?

2. Judging from these notes, how would you describe Prather as a person? How many people do you think have these same feelings?

3. What value do you think keeping this journal had for Prather? Do you think that keeping a journal would help you deal with the people and problems in your life? Why or why not?

"No one in the world was as strong, or as wise, as his father."

Lois Dykeman Kleihauer

THE CUB

● Most children have a special, complicated relationship with a parent of their own sex — boys with their fathers, girls with their mothers. Competition often gets mixed up with love, especially at the age when the child is trying to become an adult. How does a parent handle this? How does a kid handle it? This story shows how both sides feel.

ONE OF HIS FIRST MEMORIES WAS OF HIS father bending down from his great height to sweep him into the air. Up he went, gasping and laughing with delight. He could look down on his mother's upturned face as she watched, laughing with them, and at the thick shock of his father's brown hair, and at his white teeth.

Then he would come down, shrieking happily, but he was never afraid, not with his father's hands holding him. No one in the world was as strong, or as wise, as his father.

He remembered a time when his father moved the piano across the room for his mother. He watched while she guided it into its new position, and he saw the difference in their hands as they rested, side by side, upon the gleaming walnut. His mother's hands were white and slim and delicate, his father's large and square and strong.

As he grew, he learned to play bear. When it was time for his father to come home at night, he would lurk behind the kitchen door. When he heard the closing of the garage door, he would hold his breath and squeeze himself into the crack behind the door. Then he would be quiet.

It was always the same. His father would open the door and stand there, the backs of his long legs deceptively close. "Where's the boy?"

He would glance at the conspiratorial[1] smile on his mother's face, and then he would leap and grab his father about the knees, and his father would look down and shout, "Hey, what's this? A bear — a young cub!"

Then, no matter how tightly he tried to cling, he was lifted up and perched upon his father's shoulder, and they would march past his mother, and together they would duck their heads beneath the doors.

And then he went to school. And on the playground, he learned how to wrestle and shout, how to hold back tears, how to get a half-nelson on the boy who tried to take his football away from him. He came home at night and practiced his new wisdom on his father. Straining and puffing, he tried to pull his father off the lounge chair while his father kept on reading the paper, only glancing up now and then to ask in wild wonderment, "What are you trying to do, boy?"

He would stand and look at his father. "Gee whiz, Dad!" And then he would realize that his father was teasing him, and he would crawl up on his father's lap and pummel him in affectionate frustration.

And still he grew — taller, slimmer, stronger. He was like a young buck, with tiny new horns. He wanted to lock them with any other young buck's, to test them in combat. He measured his biceps with his mother's tape measure. Exultantly, he thrust his arm in front of his father. "Feel that! How's that for muscle?"

His father put his great thumb into the flexed muscle and pressed, and the boy pulled back, protesting, laughing. "Ouch!"

Sometimes they wrestled on the floor together, and his mother moved the chairs back. "Be careful, Charles — don't hurt him."

After a while his father would push him aside and sit in his chair, his long legs thrust out before him, and the boy would scramble to his feet, half-resentful, half-mirthful over the ease with which his father mastered him.

"Doggone it, Dad, someday — " he would say.

He went out for football and track in high school. He surprised even himself now, there was so much more of him. And he could look down on his mother. "Little one," he called her, or "small fry."

Sometimes he took her wrists and backed her into a chair, while he laughed and she scolded. "I'll — I'll take you across my knee."

"Who will?" he demanded.

"Well — your father still can," she said.

His father — well, that was different.

They still wrestled occasionally, but it distressed his mother. She hovered about them, worrying, unable to comprehend the need for their struggling. It always ended the same way, with the boy upon his back prostrate,[2] and his father grinning down at him. "Give?"

"Give." And he got up, shaking his head.

"I wish you wouldn't," his mother would say, fretting. "There's no point in it. You'll hurt yourselves; don't do it anymore."

So for nearly a year they had not wrestled, but he thought about it one night at dinner. He looked at his father closely. It was queer, but his father didn't look nearly as tall or broad-shouldered as he used to. He could even look his father straight in the eyes now.

"How much do you weigh, Dad?" he asked.

His father threw him a mild glance. "About the same; about a hundred and ninety. Why?"

The boy grinned. "Just wondering."

But after a while he went over to his father where he sat reading the paper and took it out of his hands. His father glanced up, his eyes at first questioning and then narrowing to meet the challenge in his son's. "So," he said, softly.

"Come on, Dad."

His father took off his coat and began to unbutton his shirt.

His mother came in from the kitchen, alarmed. "Oh, Charles! Bill! Don't — you'll hurt yourselves!" But they paid no attention to her. They were standing now, their shirts off. They watched each other, intent and purposeful. The boy's teeth gleamed again. They circled for a moment, and then their hands closed upon each other's arms.

They strained against each other, and then the boy went down, taking his father with him. They moved and writhed and turned, in silence seeking an advantage, in silence pressing it to its conclusion. There was the sound of the thumps of their bodies upon the rug and of the quick, hard intake of breath. The boy showed his teeth occasionally in a grimace of pain. His mother stood at one side, both hands pressed against her ears. Occasionally her lips moved, but she did not make a sound.

After a while the boy pinned his father on his back. "Give!" he demanded.

His father said, "Heck, no!" And with great effort he pushed the boy off, and the struggle began again.

But at the end his father lay prostrate, and a look of bewilderment came into his eyes. He struggled desperately against his son's merciless, restraining hands. Finally he lay quiet, only his chest heaving, his breath coming loudly.

The boy said, "Give!"

The man frowned, shaking his head.

Still the boy knelt on him, pinning him down.

"Give!" he said, and tightened his grip. "Give!"

All at once his father began to laugh, silently, his shoulders shaking. The boy felt his mother's fingers tugging fiercely at his shoulder. "Let him up," she said. "Let him up!"

The boy looked down at his father. "Give up?"

His father stopped laughing, but his eyes were still wet. "Okay," he said. "I give."

The boy stood up and reached a hand to his father to help him up, but his mother was before him, putting an arm about his father's shoulders, helping him to rise. They stood together and looked at him, his father grinning gamely, his mother with baffled pain in her eyes.

The boy started to laugh. "I guess I — " He stopped. "Gosh, Dad, I didn't hurt you, did I?"

"Heck, no, I'm all right. Next time . . . "

"Yeah, maybe next time . . . "

And his mother did not contradict what they said, for she knew as well as they that there would never be a next time.

For a moment the three of them stood looking at one another, and then, suddenly, blindly, the boy turned. He ran through the door under which he had ducked so many times when he had ridden on his father's shoulders. He went out the kitchen door, behind which he had hidden, waiting to leap out and pounce upon his father's legs.

It was dark outside. He stood on the steps, feeling the air cool against his sweaty body. He stood with lifted head, looking at the stars, and then he could not see them because of the tears that burned his eyes and ran down his cheeks.

[1] **conspiratorial:** suggesting a conspiracy or secret plot
[2] **prostrate:** lying down flat and helpless

A CLOSER LOOK

1. Why does the son decide to wrestle his father? How is this wrestling match different from all the ones they had had before?

2. How does the mother react to this fight? Why? How do you think the father feels afterward? How do you think the son feels? Why?

3. In what other ways might a son and a father measure themselves against each other? In what ways might a daughter and mother compete? Do you think this competition is good for them? Why or why not?

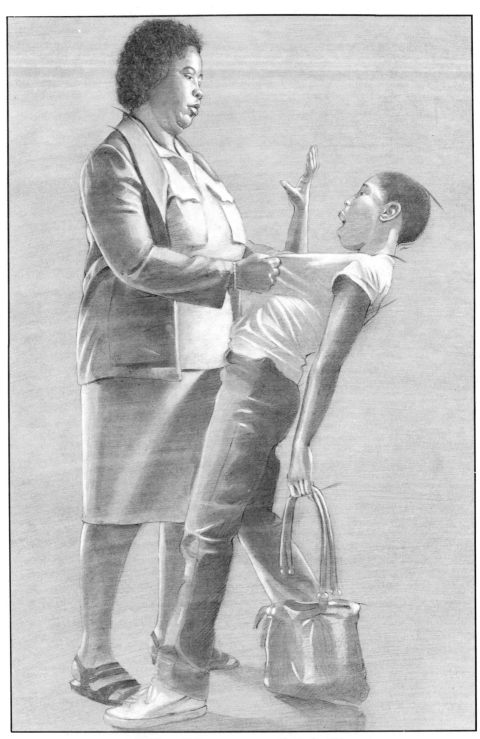

"What did you want to do it for?"

Langston Hughes

THANK YOU, M'AM

● In this story, a boy named Roger wants something so badly that he's willing to steal to get it. Thanks to a woman named Mrs. Jones, however, Roger gets far more than the money he wanted. She gives him what he really needs — trust, kindness, and self-respect.

SHE WAS A LARGE WOMAN WITH A LARGE PURSE that had everything in it but a hammer and nails. It had a long strap, and she carried it slung across her shoulder. It was about eleven o'clock at night, dark, and she was walking alone, when a boy ran up behind her and tried to snatch her purse. The strap broke with the sudden single tug the boy gave it from behind. But the boy's weight and the weight of the purse combined caused him to lose his balance. Instead of taking off full blast as he had hoped, the boy fell on his back on the sidewalk, and his legs flew up. The large woman simply turned around and kicked him right square in his blue-jeaned sitter. Then she reached down, picked the boy up by his shirt front, and shook him until his teeth rattled.

After that the woman said, ''Pick up my pocketbook, boy, and give it here.''

She still held him tightly. But she bent down enough to permit him to stoop and pick up her purse. Then she said, ''Now ain't you ashamed of yourself?''

151

Firmly gripped by his shirt front, the boy said, "Yes'm."

The woman said, "What did you want to do it for?"

The boy said, "I didn't aim to."

She said, "You a lie!"

By that time two or three people passed, stopped, turned to look, and some stood watching.

"If I turn you loose, will you run?" asked the woman.

"Yes'm," said the boy.

"Then I won't turn you loose," said the woman. She did not release him.

"Lady, I'm sorry," whispered the boy.

"Um-hum! Your face is dirty. I got a great mind to wash your face for you. Ain't you got nobody home to tell you to wash your face?"

"No'm," said the boy.

"Then it will get washed this evening," said the large woman, starting up the street, dragging the frightened boy behind her.

He looked as if he was fourteen or fifteen, frail and willow-wild, in tennis shoes and blue jeans.

The woman said, "You ought to be my son. I would teach you right from wrong. Least I can do right now is to wash your face. Are you hungry?"

"No'm," said the being-dragged boy. "I just want you to turn me loose."

"Was I bothering *you* when I turned that corner?" asked the woman.

"No'm."

"But you put yourself in contact with *me*," said the woman. "If you think that that contact is not going to last awhile, you got another thought coming. When I get through with you, sir, you are going to remember Mrs. Luella Bates Washington Jones."

Sweat popped out on the boy's face and he began to struggle. Mrs. Jones stopped, jerked him around in front of her, put a half nelson about his neck, and continued to drag him up the street. When she got to her door, she dragged the boy inside, down a hall, and into a large kitchenette-furnished room at the rear of the house. She switched on the light and left the door open. The boy could hear other roomers laughing and talking in the large house. Some of their doors were open, too, so he knew he and the woman were not alone. The woman still had him by the neck in the middle of her room.

"You gonna take me to jail?"

She said, "What is your name?"

"Roger," answered the boy.

"Then, Roger, you go to that sink and wash your face," said the woman, whereupon she turned him loose — at last. Roger looked at the door — looked at the woman — looked at the door — *and went to the sink.*

"Let the water run until it gets warm," she said. "Here's a clean towel."

"You gonna take me to jail?" asked the boy, bending over the sink.

"Not with that face, I would not take you nowhere," said the woman. "Here I am trying to get home to cook me a bite to eat, and you snatch my pocketbook! Maybe you ain't been to your supper either, late as it be. Have you?"

"There's nobody home at my house," said the boy.

"Then we'll eat," said the woman. "I believe you're hungry — or been hungry — to try to snatch my pocketbook!"

"I want a pair of suede shoes," said the boy.

"Well, you didn't have to snatch *my* pocketbook to get some suede shoes," said Mrs. Luella Bates Washington Jones. "You could of asked me.''

"M'am?''

The water dripping from his face, the boy looked at her. There was a long pause. A very long pause. After he had dried his face and not knowing what else to do, dried it again, the boy turned around, wondering what next. The door was open. He could make a dash for it down the hall. He could run, run, run, *run!*

The woman was sitting on the day bed. After a while she said, "I were young once and I wanted things I could not get.''

There was another long pause. The boy's mouth opened. Then he frowned, not knowing he frowned.

The woman said, "Um-hum! You thought I was going to say *but*, didn't you? You thought I was going to say, *but I didn't snatch people's pocketbooks.* Well, I wasn't going to say that.'' Pause. Silence. "I have done things, too, which I would not tell you, son — neither tell God, if He didn't already know. Everybody's got something in common. So you set down while I fix us something to eat. You might run that comb through your hair so you will look presentable.''

In another corner of the room behind a screen was a gas plate and an icebox. Mrs. Jones got up and went behind the screen. The woman did not watch the boy to see if he was going to run now, nor did she watch her purse, which she left behind her on the day bed. But the boy took care to sit on the far side of the room, away from the purse, where he thought she could easily see him out of the corner of her eye if she wanted to. He did not trust the woman *not* to trust him. And he did not want to be mistrusted now.

"Do you need somebody to go to the store,'' asked the boy, "maybe to get some milk or something?''

"Don't believe I do,'' said the woman, "unless you just want sweet milk yourself. I was going to make cocoa out of this canned milk I got here.''

"That will be fine,'' said the boy.

She heated some lima beans and ham she had in the icebox, made the cocoa, and set the table. The woman did not ask the boy anything about where he lived, or his folks, or anything else that would embarrass him. Instead, as they ate, she told him about her job in a hotel beauty shop that stayed open late, what the work was like, and how all kinds of women came in and out, blondes, redheads, and Spanish. Then she cut him a half of her ten-cent cake.

"Eat some more, son," she said.

When they were finished eating, she got up and said, "Now here, take this ten dollars and buy yourself some suede shoes. And next time, do not make the mistake of latching onto *my* pocketbook *nor nobody else's* — because shoes got by devilish ways will burn your feet. I got to get my rest now. But from here on in, son, I hope you will behave yourself."

She led him down the hall to the front door and opened it. "Good night! Behave yourself, boy!" she said, looking out into the street as he went down the steps.

The boy wanted to say something other than, "Thank you, m'am," to Mrs. Luella Bates Washington Jones, but although his lips moved, he couldn't even say that as he turned at the foot of the barren stoop and looked up at the large woman in the door. Then she shut the door.

•

A CLOSER LOOK

1. Why does Roger try to steal Mrs. Jones' pocketbook? How does she react to his effort?

2. Roger has an opportunity to run away from Mrs. Jones, but doesn't. Why?

3. Should Mrs. Jones have given Roger the money? Why or why not? Do you think the boy's experience with Mrs. Jones will change him? Why or why not?

● In order to grow and blossom, flowers need strong roots. Are children any different? When Children "Blossom," perhaps they should remember the support they got from their parents along the way.

Marilou Awiakta

MOTHEROOT

Creation often
needs two hearts
one to root
and one to flow
One to sustain
in time of drought
and hold fast
against winds of pain
the fragile bloom
that in the glory
of its hour
affirms a heart
unsung, unseen.

"You can learn to play it. You're somebody, Jim."

Kurt Vonnegut

THE KID NOBODY COULD HANDLE

● Teachers play an important role in our lives — particularly those who take a special interest is us and make us feel we matter. This is the story of a boy headed for a lifetime of failure — until he meets a teacher who cares.

IT WAS SEVEN-THIRTY IN THE MORNING. WADDLING, clanking, muddy machines were tearing a hill to pieces behind a restaurant. Trucks were hauling the pieces away. Inside the restaurant, dishes rattled on their shelves. Tables quaked. A very kind man with a headful of music looked down at the jiggling yolks of his breakfast eggs. His wife was visiting relatives out of town. He was on his own.

The kind man was George M. Helmholtz, a man of forty, head of the music department of Lincoln High School, and director of the band. Life had treated him well. Each year he dreamed the same big dream. He dreamed of leading as fine a band as there was on the face of the earth. And each year the dream came true.

It came true because Helmholtz was sure that a man couldn't have a better dream than his. Faced by his unnerving sureness, Kiwanians, Rotarians, and Lions paid for band uniforms that cost twice as much as their best suits. School administrators let Helmholtz raid the budget for expensive props, and youngsters played their hearts out for him. When youngsters had no talent, Helmholtz made them play on guts alone.

Everything was good about Helmholtz's life except his finances. He was so dazzled by his big dream that he was a child in the marketplace. Ten years before, he had sold the hill behind the restaurant to Bert Quinn, the restaurant owner, for one thousand dollars. It was now apparent, even to Helmholtz, that Helmholtz had been had.

Quinn sat down in the booth with the bandmaster. He was a bachelor, a small, dark, humorless man. He wasn't a well man. He couldn't sleep, he couldn't stop working, he couldn't smile warmly. He had only two moods: one suspicious and self-pitying, the other arrogant and boastful. The first mood applied when he was losing money. The second mood applied when he was making it.

Quinn was in the arrogant and boastful mood when he sat down with Helmholtz. He sucked whistlingly on a toothpick, and talked of vision — his own.

"I wonder how many eyes saw the hill before I did?" said Quinn. "Thousands and thousands, I'll bet — and not one saw what I saw. How many eyes?"

"Mine, at least," said Helmholtz. All the hill had meant to him was a panting climb, free blackberries, taxes, and a place for band picnics.

"You inherit the hill from your old man, and it's nothing but a pain in the neck to you," said Quinn. "So you figure you'll stick me with it."

"I didn't figure to stick you," Helmholtz protested. "The price was more than fair."

"You say that now," said Quinn gleefully. "Sure, Helmholtz, you say that now. Now you see the shopping district's got to grow. Now you see what I saw."

"Yes," said Helmholtz. "Too late, too late." He looked around for some diversion, and saw a fifteen-year-old boy coming toward him, mopping the aisle between booths.

The boy was small but with tough, stringy muscles standing out on his neck and forearms. Childhood lingered in his features. But when he paused to rest, his fingers went hopefully to the silky beginnings of sideburns and a mustache. He mopped like a robot, jerkily, brainlessly, but took pains not to splash suds over the toes of his black boots.

"So what do I do when I get the hill?" said Quinn. "I tear it down, and it's like somebody pulled down a dam. All of a sudden everybody wants to build a store where the hill was."

"Um," said Helmholtz. He smiled genially at the boy. The boy looked through him without a twitch of recognition.

"We all got something," said Quinn. "You got music; I got vision." And he smiled, for it was perfectly clear to both where the money lay. "Think big!" said Quinn. "Dream big! That's what vision is. Keep your eyes wider open than anybody else's."

"That boy," said Helmholtz, "I've seen him around school, but I never knew his name."

Quinn laughed cheerlessly. "Billy the Kid? The storm trooper? Rudolph Valentino? Flash Gordon?" He called the boy . . . "Hey, Jim! Come here a minute."

Helmholtz was horrified to see that the boy's eyes were as expressionless as oysters.

"This is my brother-in-law's kid by another marriage — before he married my sister," said Quinn. "His name's Jim Donnini, and he's from the south side of Chicago. He's very tough."

Jim Donnini's hands tightened on the mop handle.

"How do you do?" said Helmholtz.

"Hi," said Jim emptily.

"He's living with me now," said Quinn. "He's my baby now."

"You want a lift to school, Jim?"

"Yeah, he wants a lift to school," said Quinn. "See what you make of him. He won't talk to me." He turned to Jim. "Go on, kid, wash up and shave."

Robotlike, Jim marched away.

"Where are his parents?"

"His mother's dead. His old man married my sister, walked out on her, and stuck her with him. Then the court didn't like the way she was raising him, and put him in foster homes for a while. Then they decided to get him clear out of Chicago, so they stuck me with him." He shook his head. "Life's a funny thing, Helmholtz."

"Not very funny, sometimes," said Helmholtz. He pushed his eggs away.

"Like some whole new race of people coming up," said Quinn wonderingly. "Nothing like the kids we got around here. He's got those boots, the black jacket — and he won't talk. He won't run around with the other kids. Won't study. I don't think he can even read and write very good."

"Does he like music at all? Or drawing? Or animals?" said Helmholtz. "Does he collect anything?"

"You know what he likes?" said Quinn. "He likes to polish those boots — get off by himself and polish those boots. And when he's really in heaven is when he can get off by himself, spread comic books all around him on the floor, polish his boots, and watch television." He smiled ruefully.[1] "Yeah, he had a collection, too. And I took it away from him and threw it in the river."

"Threw it in the river?" said Helmholtz.

"Yeah," said Quinn. "Eight knives — some with blades as long as your hand."

Helmholtz paled. "Oh." A prickling sensation spread over the back of his neck. "This is a new problem at Lincoln High. I hardly know what to think about it." He swept spilled salt together in a neat little pile, just as he would have liked to sweep together his scattered thoughts. "It's a kind of sickness, isn't it? That's the way to look at it?"

"Sick?" said Quinn. He slapped the table. "You can say that again!" He tapped his chest. "And Doctor Quinn is just the man to give him what's good for what ails him."

"What's that?" said Helmholtz.

"No more talk about the poor little sick boy," said Quinn grimly. "That's all he's heard from the social workers and the juvenile court, and goodness knows who all. From now on, he's a no-good bum of a man. I'll ride his tail till he straightens up and flies right or winds up in the can for life. One way or the other."

"I see," said Helmholtz.

"Like listening to music?" said Helmholtz to Jim brightly, as they rode to school in Helmholtz's car.

Jim said nothing. He was stroking his mustache and sideburns, which he had not shaved off.

"Ever drum with the fingers or keep time with your feet?" said Helmholtz. He had noticed that Jim's boots were decorated with chains that had no function but to jingle as he walked.

Jim sighed with boredom.

"Or whistle?" said Helmholtz. "If you do any of those things, it's just like picking up the keys to a whole new world — a world as beautiful as any world can be."

Jim gave a soft Bronx cheer.

"Each year he dreamed the same big dream."

"There!" said Helmholtz. "You've illustrated the basic principle of the family of brass wind instruments. The glorious voice of every one of them starts with a buzz on the lips."

The seat springs of Helmholtz's old car creaked under Jim, as Jim shifted his weight. Helmholtz took this as a sign of interest, and he turned to smile in comradely fashion. But Jim had shifted his weight in order to get a cigarette from inside his tight leather jacket.

Helmholtz was too upset to comment at once. It was only at the end of the ride, as he turned into the teachers' parking lot, that he thought of something to say.

"Sometimes," said Helmholtz, "I get so lonely and disgusted, I don't see how I can stand it. I feel like doing all kinds of crazy things, just for the heck of it — things that might even be bad for me."

Jim blew a smoke ring expertly.

"And then!" said Helmholtz. He snapped his fingers and honked his horn. "And then, Jim, I remember I've got at least one tiny corner of the universe I can make just the way I want it! I can go to it and gloat over it until I'm brand-new and happy again."

"Aren't you the lucky one?" said Jim. He yawned.

163

"I am, for a fact," said Helmholtz. "My corner of the universe happens to be the air around my band. I can fill it with music. Mr. Beeler, in zoology, has his butterflies. Mr. Trottman, in physics, has his pendulum and tuning forks. Making sure everybody has a corner like that is about the biggest job we teachers have. I — "

The car door opened and slammed, and Jim was gone. Helmholtz stamped out Jim's cigarette and buried it under the gravel of the parking lot.

Helmholtz's first class of the morning was C Band, where beginners thumped and wheezed and tooted as best they could, and looked down the long, long, long road through B Band to A Band, the Lincoln High School Ten Square Band, the finest band in the world.

Helmholtz stepped onto the podium and raised his baton.

"You are better than you think," he said. "A-one, a-two, a-three." Down came the baton.

C Band set out in its quest for beauty — set out like a rusty switch engine, with valves stuck, pipes clogged, and bearings dry.

Helmholtz was still smiling at the end of the hour, because he'd heard in his mind the music as it was going to be someday. His throat was raw, for he had been singing with the band for the whole hour. He stepped into the hall for a drink from the fountain.

As he drank, he heard the jingling of chains. He looked up at Jim Donnini. Rivers of students flowed between classrooms, pausing in friendly eddies, flowing on again. Jim was alone. When he paused, it wasn't to greet anyone, but to polish the toes of his boots on his trouser legs. He had the air of a spy in a melodrama. He missed nothing, liked nothing, and looked forward to the great day when everything would be turned upside down.

"Hello, Jim," said Helmholtz. "Say, I was just thinking about you. We've got a lot of clubs and teams that meet after school. And that's a good way to get to know a lot of people."

Jim measured Helmholtz carefully with his eyes. "Maybe I don't want to know a lot of people," he said. "Ever think of that?" He set his feet down hard to make his chains jingle as he walked away.

When Helmholtz returned to the podium for a rehearsal of B Band, there was a note waiting for him, calling him to a special faculty meeting.

The meeting was about vandalism.

Someone had broken into the school and wrecked the office of

Mr. Crane, head of the English Department. The poor man's treasures — books, diplomas, snapshots of England, the beginnings of eleven novels — had been ripped and crumpled, mixed, dumped and trampled, and drenched with ink.

Helmholtz was sickened. He couldn't believe it. He couldn't bring himself to think about it. It didn't become real to him until late that night, in a dream. In the dream Helmholtz saw a boy with barracuda teeth, with claws like baling hooks. The monster climbed into a window of the high school and dropped to the floor of the band rehearsal room. The monster clawed to shreds the heads of the biggest drum in the state. Helmholtz woke up howling. There was nothing to do but dress and go to the school.

At two in the morning, Helmholtz caressed the drum heads in the band rehearsal room, with the night watchman looking on. He rolled the drum back and forth on its cart. He turned the light inside on and off, on and off. The drum was unharmed. The night watchman left to make his rounds.

The band's treasure house was safe. With the contentment of a miser counting his money, Helmholtz fondled the rest of the instruments, one by one. And then he began to polish the sousaphones. As he polished, he could hear the great horns roaring. He could see them flashing in the sunlight, with the Stars and Stripes and the banner of Lincoln High going before.

"Yump-yump, tiddle-tiddle, yump-yump, tiddle-tiddle!" sang Helmholtz happily. "Yump-yump-yump, ra-a-a-a-a, yump-yump, yump-yump — boom!"

As he paused to choose the next number for his imaginary band to play, he heard a furtive[2] noise in the chemistry laboratory next door. Helmholtz sneaked into the hall, jerked open the laboratory door, and flashed on the lights. Jim Donnini had a bottle of acid in either hand. He was splashing acid over the periodic table of the elements, over the blackboards covered with formulas, over the bust of Lavoisier. The scene was the most repulsive thing Helmholtz could have looked upon.

Jim smiled with thin bravado.

"Get out," said Helmholtz.

"What're you gonna do?" said Jim.

"Clean up. Save what I can," said Helmholtz dazedly. He picked up a wad of cotton waste and began wiping up the acid.

"Our aim is to make the world more beautiful."

"You gonna call the cops?" said Jim.

"I — I don't know," said Helmholtz. "No thoughts come. If I'd caught you hurting the bass drum, I think I would have killed you with a single blow. But I wouldn't have had any intelligent thoughts about what you were — what you thought you were doing."

"It's about time this place got set on its ear," said Jim.

"Is it?" said Helmholtz. "That must be so, if one of our students wants to murder it."

"What good is it?" said Jim.

"Not much good, I guess," said Helmholtz. "It's just the best thing human beings ever managed to do." He was helpless, talking to himself. He had a bag of tricks for making boys behave like men — tricks that played on boyish fears and dreams and loves. But here was a boy without fear, without dreams, without love.

"If you smashed up all the schools," said Helmholtz, "we wouldn't have any hope left."

"What hope?" said Jim.

"The hope that everybody will be glad he's alive," said Helmholtz. "Even you."

"That's a laugh," said Jim. "All I ever got out of this dump was a hard time. So what're you gonna do?''

"I have to do something, don't I?" said Helmholtz.

"I don't care what you do," said Jim.

"I know," said Helmholtz. "I know." He marched Jim into his tiny office off the band rehearsal room. He dialed the telephone number of the principal's home. Numbly, he waited for the bell to get the old man from his bed.

Jim dusted his boots with a rag.

Helmholtz suddenly dropped the telephone into its cradle before the principal could answer. "Isn't there anything you care about but ripping, hacking, bending, rending, smashing, bashing?" he cried. "Anything? Anything but those boots?"

"Go on! Call up whoever you're gonna call," said Jim.

Helmholtz opened a locker and took a trumpet from it. He thrust the trumpet into Jim's arms. "There!" he said, puffing with emotion. "There's my treasure. It's the dearest thing I own. I give it to you to smash. I won't move a muscle to stop you. You can have the added pleasure of watching my heart break while you do it."

Jim looked at him oddly. He laid down the trumpet.

"Go on!" said Helmholtz. "If the world has treated you so badly, it deserves to have the trumpet smashed!"

"I — " said Jim. Helmholtz grabbed his belt, put a foot behind him, and dumped him on the floor.

Helmholtz pulled Jim's boots off and threw them into a corner. "There!" said Helmholtz savagely. He jerked the boy to his feet again and thrust the trumpet into his arms once more.

Jim Donnini was barefoot now. He had lost his socks with his boots. The boy looked down. The feet that had once seemed big black clubs were narrow as chicken wings now — bony and blue, and not quite clean.

The boy shivered, then quaked. Each quake seemed to shake something loose inside, until at last there was no boy left. No boy at all. Jim's head lolled, as though he waited only for death.

Helmholtz was overwhelmed by remorse. He threw his arms around the boy. "Jim! Jim — listen to me, boy!"

Jim stopped quaking.

"You know what you've got there — the trumpet?" said Helmholtz. "You know what's special about it?"

Jim only sighed.

"It belonged to John Philip Sousa!" said Helmholtz. He rocked

167

and shook Jim gently, trying to bring him back to life. "I'll trade it to you, Jim — for your boots. It's yours, Jim! John Philip Sousa's trumpet is yours! It's worth hundreds of dollars, Jim — thousands!"

Jim laid his head on Helmholtz's breast.

"It's better than boots, Jim," said Helmholtz. "You can learn to play it. You're somebody, Jim. You're the boy with John Philip Sousa's trumpet!"

Helmholtz released Jim slowly, sure the boy would topple. Jim didn't fall. He stood alone. The trumpet was still in his arms.

"I'll take you home, Jim," said Helmholtz. "Be a good boy and I won't say a word about tonight. Polish your trumpet, and learn to be a good boy."

"Can I have my boots?" said Jim dully.

"No," said Helmholtz. "I don't think they're good for you."

He drove Jim home. He opened the car windows and the air seemed to refresh the boy. He let him out at Quinn's restaurant. The soft pats of Jim's bare feet on the sidewalk echoed down the empty street. He climbed through a window, and into his bedroom behind the kitchen. And all was still.

The next morning the waddling, clanking, muddy machines were making the vision of Bert Quinn come true. They were smoothing off the place where the hill had been behind the restaurant. They were making it as level as a billiard table.

Helmholtz sat in a booth again. Quinn joined him again. Jim mopped again. Jim kept his eyes down, refusing to notice Helmholtz. And he didn't seem to care when a surf of suds broke over the toes of his small and narrow brown Oxfords.

"Eating out two mornings in a row?" said Quinn. "Something wrong at home?"

"My wife's still out of town," said Helmholtz.

"While the cat's away — " said Quinn. He winked.

"When the cat's away," said Helmholtz, "this mouse gets lonesome."

Quinn leaned forward. "Is that why you got out of bed in the middle of the night, Helmholtz? Loneliness?" He jerked his head at Jim. "Kid! Go get Mr. Helmholtz his horn."

Jim raised his head, and Helmholtz saw that his eyes were oysterlike again. He marched away to get the trumpet.

Quinn now showed that he was excited and angry. "You take

168

away his boots and give him a horn, and I'm not supposed to get curious?'' he said. ''I'm not supposed to start asking questions? I'm not supposed to find out you caught him taking the school apart? You'd make a lousy crook, Helmholtz. You'd leave your baton, sheet music, and your driver's license at the scene of the crime.''

''I don't think about hiding clues,'' said Helmholtz. ''I just do what I do. I was going to tell you.''

Quinn's feet danced and his shoes squeaked like mice.

''Yes?'' he said. ''Well, I've got some news for you, too.''

''What is that?'' said Helmholtz uneasily.

''It's all over with Jim and me,'' said Quinn. ''Last night was the payoff. I'm sending him back where he came from.''

''To another string of foster homes?'' said Helmholtz weakly.

''Whatever the experts figure out to do with a kid like that.'' Quinn sat back, exhaled noisily, and went limp with relief.

''You can't,'' said Helmholtz.

''I can,'' said Quinn.

''That will be the end of him,'' said Helmholtz. ''He can't stand to be thrown away like that one more time.''

''He can't feel anything,'' said Quinn. ''I can't help him; I can't hurt him. Nobody can. There isn't a nerve in him.''

''A bundle of scar tissue,'' said Helmholtz.

The bundle of scar tissue returned with the trumpet. Impassively, he laid it on the table in front of Helmholtz.

Helmholtz forced a smile. ''It's yours, Jim,'' he said. ''I gave it to you.''

''Take it while you got the chance, Helmholtz,'' said Quinn. ''He doesn't want it. All he'll do is swap it for a knife or a pack of cigarettes.''

''He doesn't know what it is, yet,'' said Helmholtz. ''It takes a while to find out.''

''Is it any good?'' said Quinn.

''Any good?'' said Helmholtz, not believing his ears. ''Any good?'' He didn't see how anyone could look at the instrument and not be warmed and dazzled by it. ''Any good?'' he murmured. ''It belonged to John Philip Sousa.''

Quinn blinked stupidly. ''Who?''

Helmholtz's hands fluttered on the table top like the wings of a dying bird. ''Who was John Philip Sousa?'' he piped. No more words came. The subject was too big for a tired man to cover. The dying bird expired[3] and lay still.

After a long silence, Helmholtz picked up the trumpet. He kissed the cold mouthpiece and pumped the valves in a dream of a brilliant cadenza.[4] Over the bell of the instrument, Helmholtz saw Jim Donnini's face. It seemed to float in space — all but deaf and blind. Now Helmholtz saw the futility of men and their treasures. He had thought that his greatest treasure, the trumpet, could buy a soul for Jim. The trumpet was worthless.

Deliberately, Helmholtz hammered the trumpet against the table edge. He bent it around a coat tree. He handed the wreck to Quinn.

"Ya busted it," said Quinn, amazed. "Why'dja do that? What's that prove?"

"I — I don't know," said Helmholtz. A terrible blasphemy rumbled deep in him, like the warning of a volcano. And then, irresistibly, out it came. "Life is no good," said Helmholtz. His face twisted as he fought back tears and shame.

Helmholtz, the mountain that walked like a man, was falling apart. Jim Donnini's eyes filled with pity and alarm. They came alive. They became human. Helmholtz had got a message through. Quinn looked at Jim, and something like hope flickered for the first time in his bitterly lonely old face.

Two weeks later, a new semester began at Lincoln High.

In the band rehearsal room, the members of C Band were waiting for their leader — were waiting for their destinies as musicians to unfold.

Helmholtz stepped onto the podium, and rattled his baton against his music stand. "The Voices of Spring," he said. "Everybody hear that? The Voices of Spring?"

There were rustling sounds as the musicians put the music on their stands. In the silence that followed, Helmholtz glanced at Jim Donnini, who sat on the last seat of the worst trumpet section of the worst band in school.

His trumpet, John Philip Sousa's trumpet, George M. Helmholtz's trumpet, had been repaired.

"Think of it this way," said Helmholtz. "Our aim is to make the world more beautiful than it was when we came into it. It can be done. You can do it."

A small cry of despair came from Jim Donnini. It was meant to be private, but it pierced every ear with its poignancy.[5]

"How?" said Jim.

"Love yourself," said Helmholtz, "and make your instrument sing about it. A-one, a-two, a-three." Down came his baton.

[1] **ruefully:** with sympathy or regret
[2] **furtive:** secret; done by stealth
[3] **expired:** died
[4] **cadenza:** in music, a flourish or improvised solo passage
[5] **poignancy:** quality of being moving or touching

A CLOSER LOOK

1. What kind of life has Jim led before he meets Mr. Helmholtz? How does Jim react to Mr. Helmholtz? How does he react to Lincoln High School?

2. What do Jim's boots mean to him? What does Helmholtz's trumpet mean to him? Why do you think Helmholtz smashes his trumpet? How does this affect Jim?

3. Think of the best teacher you have ever had. What made him or her a good teacher for you? What was the most important thing you learned from him or her?

• Our finest relationships are not always with people. A loyal pet can become as important a member of the family as any human being; indeed, animals can be even better companions in some ways than humans. In this poem, Jeffers imagines what his well-loved dog would say if he were still alive.

Robinson Jeffers

THE HOUSE DOG'S GRAVE

I've changed my ways a little; I cannot now
Run with you in the evenings along the shore,
Except in a kind of dream; and you, if you dream a moment,
You see me there.

So leave awhile the paw-marks on the front door
Where I used to scratch to go out or in,
And you'd soon open; leave on the kitchen floor
The marks of my drinking-pan.

I cannot lie by your fire as I used to do
On the warm stone,
Nor at the foot of your bed; no, all the nights through
I lie alone.

But your kind thought has laid me less than six feet
Outside your window where firelight so often plays,
And where you sit to read — and I fear often grieving for me —
Every night your lamplight lies on my place.

You, man and woman, live so long, it is hard
To think of you ever dying.

A little dog would get tired, living so long.
I hope that when you are lying

Under the ground like me your lives will appear
As good and joyful as mine.
No, dears, that's too much hope: you are not so well cared for
As I have been.

And never have known the passionate undivided
Fidelities[1] that I knew.
Your minds are perhaps too active, too many-sided . . .
But to me you were true.

You were never masters, but friends. I was your friend.
I loved you well, and was loved. Deep love endures
To the end and far past the end. If this is my end,
I am not lonely. I am not afraid. I am still yours.

[1] **fidelities:** acts of loyalty and faithfulness

"But the tree was replanted and it grew."

Linda Marasco

THE TREE

• As the years pass, relationships within a family change. This story looks at a family that is going off in many new directions — and reveals what holds them together still.

IT WAS AT SUPPER THAT FATHER TOLD US ABOUT the tree. "Saturday," he said in his authoritative voice, "we move the tree." Everyone stopped and turned to Father. "The tree with the scar," he said. "The one in the back. We'll move it to the front." Everyone was still looking at Father. He broke a piece of bread and dipped it in the moat of gravy around his potatoes.

Joe was the first to speak. He picked up his glass and twisted it in his hands, intently studying the liquid as it swirled. He cleared his throat.

"Eddie and I thought we might take the car over to the station Saturday and put it on the lift. I want to check the left rear tire, and that's the only day we can have the rack."

He looked up from his glass. Father nodded.

Mickey dropped his fork. "I won't be around either," he said. "Mark and I are going out to Freeport."

No one spoke.

"It's the first day off I've had in two weeks," he went on. "It's only fair that . . .'' Then he stopped. Everyone was looking at Father.

"All right," he said. "Saturday is my day off, too, but all right." He looked at Diane and me. Diane stared back.

"I'm going to the movies with Fran," she began defensively. "I asked on Tuesday." She got up from the table and took her plate into the kitchen.

Father looked at me. "What about you?" he asked. "What are you doing Saturday?"

I looked down at my potatoes. They were pretty lumpy.

"Joanne and I were going to play tennis."

Diane entered the room, her dark ponytail swaying mischievously. "I thought you said Joanne was upstate for the week," she said.

I turned around and shot her a look.

"Oh, THAT Joanne!" exclaimed Diane, almost dropping the teapot.

"All right," said Father, "then I'll do it myself."

Mickey squirmed in his chair. Nobody touched his food except my father. Mother was the first to break the quiet as she poured herself a cup of tea.

As the steam rose, she sighed and absently stared into the mist.

"Gee," she said as she raised and lowered the teabag in the cup. "When I think of that tree. . . . How old is it, Andy? Must be seventeen, eighteen, years old. I remember you bought four trees when Joe was about two."

The teabag was beginning to look sick.

"Now that I think about it, it was kind of silly — putting them on the side of the house, I mean. There wasn't even dirt there — just sand. It's amazing how they ever grew."

She put down the teabag and began to stir without looking at the cup.

"But they grew," she sighed.

She reached for the sugar bowl and unconsciously poured a teaspoonful of sugar into the cup.

"And I remember when the car hit the tree. The tree was completely uprooted and lying on the ground. The bark had been sheared off and there was a big gash running up the length of the trunk.

"But the tree was replanted and it grew."

She put another teaspoonful of sugar into the cup. Then she laid down her spoon and looked up. "Did I put any sugar in my tea?" she asked.

Father had finished eating. He carefully wiped his mouth and put down his napkin. "Saturday," he said. "Saturday I'll move the tree." The matter was settled.

It was not until Saturday that I remembered about the tree. I was lying on my bed reading when I heard the sound of hard metal hitting the soil. I went to the back window and looked out at the bent figure of my father digging up the tree. Joe came and stood beside me.

"Some people sure are stubborn," he said.

"Yeah," I answered.

I went back to my bed and plunked myself down to finish my reading. All I could hear was the sound of my father's shoveling. I rolled off my bed and went down the stairs.

Diane was sitting on the back steps with her head in her hands. Her ponytail was drooping.

"Weren't you going to the movies?" I asked.

"What happened to Joanne?" she answered.

We watched the boys as they came out of the house and went into the garage. Both came out with shovels.

Father neither looked up nor said a word. Diane and I brought the wheelbarrow over as the boys began to shovel.

"Stupid tree," Joe muttered.

Father smiled.

The tree would live, I thought.

A CLOSER LOOK

1. List the various members of the family and their reasons for not being home on Saturday. Using evidence in the story, try to guess how old each child is.

2. Why do you think the children all had something else to do on Saturday? Why did they help their father in the end?

3. Why will the tree live? What else is going to "live"?

● Grandparents often have a strong sense of who they are, and what they want from life. Is it because life was harder then, and therefore more rewarding? If only we could learn the secret of their strength!

Margaret Walker

LINEAGE

My grandmothers were strong.
They followed plows and bent to toil.
They moved through fields sowing seed.
They touched earth and grain grew.
They were full of sturdiness and singing.
My grandmothers were strong.

My grandmothers are full of memories
Smelling of soap and onions and wet clay
With veins rolling roughly over quick hands.
They have many clean words to say.
My grandmothers were strong.
Why am I not as they?

"He taught life."

Andy Rooney

HERBERT HAHN

● In newpapers and on television, Andy Rooney comments upon modern American life. He writes from the point of view of the ordinary person in the street, and offers his personal opinion of events. In this brief essay, he reminds us that teachers play an important role in our lives, and that the vision of a great teache nourishes us throughout life.

HE LIVED ONLY A THIRTY-FIVE-CENT PHONE call away, but I never called him. No one influenced my life more than he did. Now he's gone and I don't think I ever told him.

I worked late yesterday and didn't get home until after eight. My family and I had a quick dinner. It was too late to start anything else, so at ten I got to bed with the newspaper I'd never taken the time to read. The economic news was bad and the Giants' coach said he wasn't discouraged. I leafed through to the obituary[1] page and my eye caught the little headline in bold face type:

HERBERT HAHN, 75
ENGLISH TEACHER

I dropped the paper to the floor next to the bed and stared at the ceiling. Mr. Hahn was dead. *Why* hadn't I called him? I was surprised to find myself crying. I hadn't really seen Mr. Hahn for forty years. I didn't even know he was "Dr. Hahn" now, but I had

181

thought of him on almost every one of the days of those forty years.

My memory of exactly what he was like in school was incredibly clear to me. I remember every mannerism,[2] the way he pulled at the crease at the knee of his pants when he sat on the edge of his desk. I even remember that he had only two suits in 1936. One was his old suit and one was his good suit. He wore the old one for two days every other week when the good one was at the cleaners. He made only twenty-seven hundred dollars a year teaching history in Albany, New York, then, and clothes were not a top priority of his.

He left Albany in about 1945 to teach at a good private school in New Jersey, and I wasn't surprised that the obituary called him an English teacher. It didn't really matter what Mr. Hahn's class was called. He taught life, and his subject was of secondary importance. When we were fourteen and fifteen, he talked to us as though we were human beings, not children. He talked about *everything* in class. Just to make sure we knew he didn't think he was omnipotent,[3] he often followed some pronouncement[4] he'd made about government or politics by saying, "And don't forget you heard it from the same teacher who predicted in 1932 that Hitler would get nowhere in Germany."

How many teachers do you have in your life? I lay there wondering last night. Between grade school, high school, and college, if you're lucky enough to go to college, I suppose you have about fifty teachers. Is that about right?

I don't remember much about some of mine, and nothing about what they were trying to teach me. But of those fifty, I had five who were very good and two who were great. Mr. Hahn was one of those.

He didn't do a lot of extra talking, but when he talked he was direct and often brilliant. He was the only genuine philosopher I ever knew. He wasn't a teacher of philosophy, but a living, breathing philosophizer. He exuded[5] wisdom, concern for the world, and quite often a bad temper. Idiots irritated him, and it annoyed him when teenagers acted younger than he was treating them.

I went to the service for him today. I don't know why, really. There was no one there I knew, and one phone call over the years would have meant more to him. A minister spoke, but it was standard stuff, and Mr. Hahn was not what most people would call a religious person, even though he wrote a book called *The Great Religions: Interpretations.*

A young woman who taught with him spoke, and she brought the tears back to my eyes. He had touched her life in the 1970s as he had touched mine in the 1930s.

Mr. Hahn could have taught at any college in the country, but he chose to stay at the secondary level. He didn't think teaching college-age people was any more important than teaching boys and girls fourteen to eighteen. He was the kind of person who gave teachers the right to be proud to be teachers.

I just wish I had called or written to tell him how much he meant to my life.

[1] **obituary:** announcement of someone's death
[2] **mannerism:** usual way of behaving; typical gesture
[3] **omnipotent:** having unlimited power; godlike
[4] **pronouncement:** an authoritative announcement
[5] **exuded:** showed in great abundance; oozed

A CLOSER LOOK

1. What makes Rooney stop to think about Herbert Hahn? What does Rooney regret not doing?

2. What details does Rooney give you that make Herbert Hahn "come to life" for you? Why do you think Rooney considers Hahn a great teacher?

3. Make up your own list of the qualities you feel a great teacher would have? What is the most important thing a teacher can pass on to his or her students?

• Each person is the center of his or her own unique, complex web of relationships. This poem describes several different people on a rather ordinary summer night. Each person in the poem moves along his or her separate path, and yet all are connected. In spite of the matter-of-fact tone of the poem, a sense of wonder quietly grows here, verse by verse.

Lisa Hirschboeck

AUNT SARAH DIED ONE SUMMER NIGHT

Aunt Sarah died on a wicker chair on the porch one
    summer night with a cold lemonade and a Japanese
    fan and a dozen night bugs dancing around the 60
    watt bulb.

While the crickets chattered in the lawn,
    and the dog scratched and bit at his fur
    and the big black horsefly buzzed around the
    ceiling in our hot sticky kitchen.

While Mat and I kicked off our sneakers
    and ran over the wet grass, grabbing at the night
    for fireflies.

While Mary and her beau sat under the silver
    maple with leaves as big as hands, just watching
    the sky and saying nothing.

While the bullfrogs hidden in the cattails
    belched from swelling up with too much
    summer air.

Aunt Sarah died and the wind stroked her white curls,
    and a thrush perched on the highest branch sang
    her very favorite song, and the moon shone bright
    so she wouldn't stumble going up the golden
    stairs to heaven.

"In search of my mother's garden, I found my own."

Alice Walker

IN SEARCH OF
OUR MOTHERS' GARDENS

● What makes a garden grow and flourish? The same things that make our lives rich and full: hard work, a belief in possibilities, and a love of beauty. It was these qualities that Alice Walker learned from her mother.

N THE LATE 1920s, MY MOTHER RAN AWAY FROM home to marry my father. Marriage, if not running away, was expected of seventeen-year-old girls. By the time she was twenty, she had two children and was pregnant with a third. Five children later, I was born. And this is how I came to know my mother: she seemed a large, soft, loving-eyed woman who was rarely impatient in our home. Her quick, violent temper was on view only a few times a year, when she battled with the white landlord who had the misfortune to suggest to her that her children did not need to go to school.

She made all the clothes we wore, even my brothers' overalls. She made all the towels and sheets we used. She spent the summers canning vegetables and fruits. She spent the winter evenings making quilts enough to cover all our beds.

During the "working" day, she labored beside — not behind — my father in the fields. Her day began before sunup, and did not end until late at night. There was never a moment for her to sit down, undisturbed, to unravel[1] her own private thoughts; never a time free from interruption — by work or the noisy inquiries of her many children.

The artist that was and is my mother showed itself to me only after many years. This is what I finally noticed:

Like Mem, a character in [my novel] *The Third Life of Grange Copeland*, my mother adorned with flowers whatever shabby house we were forced to live in. And not just your typical straggly country stand of zinnias,[2] either. She planted ambitious gardens — and still does — with over fifty different varieties of plants that bloom profusely[3] from early March until late November. Before she left home for the fields, she watered her flowers, chopped up the grass, and laid out new beds. When she returned from the fields she might divide clumps of bulbs, dig a cold pit, uproot and replant roses, or prune branches from her taller bushes or trees — until night came and it was too dark to see.

Whatever she planted grew as if by magic, and her fame as a grower of flowers spread over three counties. Because of her creativity with her flowers, even my memories of poverty are seen through a screen of blooms — sunflowers, petunias, roses, dahlias, forsythia, spirea, delphiniums, verbena . . . and on and on.

And I remember people coming to my mother's yard to be given cuttings from her flowers; I hear again the praise showered on her because whatever rocky soil she landed on, she turned into a garden. A garden so brilliant with colors, so original in its design, so magnificent with life and creativity, that to this day people drive by our house in Georgia — perfect strangers and imperfect strangers — and ask to stand or walk among my mother's art.

I notice that it is only when my mother is working in her flowers that she is radiant, almost to the point of being invisible — except as Creator: hand and eye. She is involved in work her soul must have, ordering the universe in the image of her personal conception of Beauty.

Her face, as she prepares the Art that is her gift, is a legacy[4] of respect she leaves to me, for all that illuminates[5] and cherishes life. She has handed down respect for the possibilities — and the will to grasp them.

For her, so hindered and intruded upon in so many ways, being an artist has still been a daily part of her life. This ability to hold on, even in very simple ways, is work Black women have done for a very long time.

Guided by my heritage of love of beauty and a respect for strength — in search of my mother's garden, I found my own.

[1] **unravel:** clear up; disentangle
[2] **zinnias:** low shrubs with showy flowers
[3] **profusely:** in great abundance
[4] **legacy:** a gift given in a will by an ancestor or someone from the past
[5] **illuminates:** brightens; clarifies

A CLOSER LOOK

1. Why do you think Alice Walker's mother planted a garden? Why was she such a successful gardener?

2. Alice Walker tells you that with her mother's help she found her own garden. What kind of garden is she referring to?

3. Would you have liked to know Alice Walker's mother? Why or why not? What would you have learned from her?

● Although this sounds like a very simple poem, it sums up one of the most amazing things about relationships — that they can change the way you feel about life.

Paul Engle

TOGETHER

Because we do
All things together
All things improve,
Even weather.

Our daily meat
And bread taste better,
Trees greener,
Rain is wetter.